THE INTERNET FOR DUMMIES®

Quick Reference
6th Edition

by John R. Levine, Arnold Reinhold, and Margaret Levine Young

IDG BOOKS WORLDWIDE

IDG Books Worldwide, Inc.
An International Data Group Company

Foster City, CA ✦ Chicago, IL ✦ Indianapolis, IN ✦ New York, NY

The Internet For Dummies® **Quick Reference, 6th Edition**

Published by
IDG Books Worldwide, Inc.
An International Data Group Company
919 E. Hillsdale Blvd.
Suite 400
Foster City, CA 94404
www.idgbooks.com (IDG Books Worldwide Web site)
www.dummies.com (Dummies Press Web site)

Library of Congress Catalog Card No.: 99-69258

ISBN: 0-7645-0675-7

Printed in the United States of America

10 9 8 7 6 5 4 3 2 1

6P/SU/QR/QQ/IN

Distributed in the United States by IDG Books Worldwide, Inc.

Distributed by CDG Books Canada Inc. for Canada; by Transworld Publishers Limited in the United Kingdom; by IDG Norge Books for Norway; by IDG Sweden Books for Sweden; by IDG Books Australia Publishing Corporation Pty. Ltd. for Australia and New Zealand; by TransQuest Publishers Pte Ltd. for Singapore, Malaysia, Thailand, Indonesia, and Hong Kong; by Gotop Information Inc. for Taiwan; by ICG Muse, Inc. for Japan; by Intersoft for South Africa; by Eyrolles for France; by International Thomson Publishing for Germany, Austria and Switzerland; by Distribuidora Cuspide for Argentina; by LR International for Brazil; by Galileo Libros for Chile; by Ediciones ZETA S.C.R. Ltda. for Peru; by WS Computer Publishing Corporation, Inc., for the Philippines; by Contemporanea de Ediciones for Venezuela; by Express Computer Distributors for the Caribbean and West Indies; by Micronesia Media Distributor, Inc. for Micronesia; by Chips Computadoras S.A. de C.V. for Mexico; by Editorial Norma de Panama S.A. for Panama; by American Bookshops for Finland.

For general information on IDG Books Worldwide's books in the U.S., please call our Consumer Customer Service department at 800-762-2974. For reseller information, including discounts and premium sales, please call our Reseller Customer Service department at 800-434-3422.

For information on where to purchase IDG Books Worldwide's books outside the U.S., please contact our International Sales department at 317-596-5530 or fax 317-572-4002.

For consumer information on foreign language translations, please contact our Customer Service department at 1-800-434-3422, fax 317-572-4002, or e-mail rights@idgbooks.com.

For information on licensing foreign or domestic rights, please phone +1-650-653-7098.

For sales inquiries and special prices for bulk quantities, please contact our Sales department at 800-762-2974 or write to the address above.

For information on using IDG Books Worldwide's books in the classroom or for ordering examination copies, please contact our Educational Sales department at 800-434-2086 or fax 317-572-4005.

For press review copies, author interviews, or other publicity information, please contact our Public Relations department at 650-653-7000 or fax 650-653-7500.

For authorization to photocopy items for corporate, personal, or educational use, please contact Copyright Clearance Center, 222 Rosewood Drive, Danvers, MA 01923, or fax 978-750-4470.

About the Authors

John R. Levine was a member of the same computer club Margy was in — before high school students, or even high schools, had computers. He wrote his first program in 1967 on an IBM 1130 (a computer almost as fast as your modern digital wristwatch, only more difficult to use). He became an official system administrator of a networked computer at Yale in 1975 and has been working in the computer and network biz since 1977. He got his company on to Usenet (see Part IV) early enough that it appears in a 1982 *Byte* magazine article in a map of Usenet, which then was so small that the map fit on half a page.

He used to spend most of his time writing software, although now he mostly writes books (including *UNIX For Dummies* and *Internet Secrets,* both from IDG Books Worldwide, Inc.) because it's more fun and he can do so at home in the hamlet of Trumansburg, New York, where he holds the exalted rank of sewer commissioner and offers free samples to visitors and plays with his young daughter when he's supposed to be writing. He also does a fair amount of public speaking. (*See* www.iecc.com/johnl.) He holds a B.A. and a Ph.D. in computer science from Yale University, but please don't hold that against him.

Arnold Reinhold has been programming computers since they had filaments. His first introduction to the hype/so what?/wow! cycle that governs the computer industry evolution was the transistor. He has gotten to do cool stuff in spacecraft guidance, air traffic control, computer-aided design, robotics, machine vision and cryptography. Arnold has been on and off the Internet for more than 15 years. He is also a coauthor of *E-Mail For Dummies* (IDG Books Worldwide). Arnold studied mathematics at CCNY and MIT and management at Harvard. You can check out his home page at www.hayom.com/reinhold.html.

Unlike her peers in that 40-something bracket, **Margaret Levine Young** was exposed to computers at an early age. In high school, she got into a computer club known as the R.E.S.I.S.T.O.R.S., a group of kids who spent Saturdays in a barn fooling around with three antiquated computers. She stayed in the field through college against her better judgment and despite her brother John's presence as a graduate student in the computer science department. Margy graduated from Yale and went on to become one of the first microcomputer managers in the early 1980s at Columbia Pictures, where she rode the elevator with big stars whose names she wouldn't dream of dropping here.

Since then, Margy (www.gurus.com/margy) has coauthored more than 20 computer books about the topics of the Internet, UNIX, WordPerfect, Microsoft Access, and (stab from the past) PC-File and Javelin, including *The Internet For Dummies,* and *WordPerfect 7 For Windows 95 For Dummies* (all from IDG Books Worldwide). She loves her husband, Jordan; her kids, Meg and Zac; gardening; chickens; reading; and anything to do with eating. Margy and her husband also run Great Tapes for Kids (www.greattapes.com) from their home in the middle of a cornfield near Middlebury, Vermont.

Authors' Acknowledgments

The authors thank the many people who created and maintain the Internet and fill it with useful information; Barbara Lapinskas, for numerous helpful suggestions and sources; Joshua Reinhold, for his patience and questions; Max and Grete Reinhold, of blessed memory; Tonia Saxon; Jordan Young; Carol Baroudi; Steve Dyer; and our ever vigilant editors, Rebecca Whitney and Colleen Totz.

In addition, we enjoy and appreciate the feedback we get from readers of *The Internet For Dummies* series. Your comments about this book help us make each edition a little better. Be sure to e-mail us, at idq6@gurus.com, and visit our Web site, at net.gurus.com.

ABOUT IDG BOOKS WORLDWIDE

Welcome to the world of IDG Books Worldwide.

IDG Books Worldwide, Inc., is a subsidiary of International Data Group, the world's largest publisher of computer-related information and the leading global provider of information services on information technology. IDG was founded more than 30 years ago by Patrick J. McGovern and now employs more than 9,000 people worldwide. IDG publishes more than 290 computer publications in over 75 countries. More than 90 million people read one or more IDG publications each month.

Launched in 1990, IDG Books Worldwide is today the #1 publisher of best-selling computer books in the United States. We are proud to have received eight awards from the Computer Press Association in recognition of editorial excellence and three from Computer Currents' First Annual Readers' Choice Awards. Our best-selling ...For Dummies® series has more than 50 million copies in print with translations in 31 languages. IDG Books Worldwide, through a joint venture with IDG's Hi-Tech Beijing, became the first U.S. publisher to publish a computer book in the People's Republic of China. In record time, IDG Books Worldwide has become the first choice for millions of readers around the world who want to learn how to better manage their businesses.

Our mission is simple: Every one of our books is designed to bring extra value and skill-building instructions to the reader. Our books are written by experts who understand and care about our readers. The knowledge base of our editorial staff comes from years of experience in publishing, education, and journalism — experience we use to produce books to carry us into the new millennium. In short, we care about books, so we attract the best people. We devote special attention to details such as audience, interior design, use of icons, and illustrations. And because we use an efficient process of authoring, editing, and desktop publishing our books electronically, we can spend more time ensuring superior content and less time on the technicalities of making books.

You can count on our commitment to deliver high-quality books at competitive prices on topics you want to read about. At IDG Books W
quality for more than 30 years. You'll find no better book on a subject than one from IDG Books Worldwide.

orldwide, we continue in the IDG tradition of delivering

John Kilcullen
Chairman and CEO
IDG Books Worldwide, Inc.

Steven Berkowitz
President and Publisher
IDG Books Worldwide, Inc.

WINNER

Eighth Annual
Computer Press
Awards ≥1992

WINNER

Ninth Annual
Computer Press
Awards ≥1993

WINNER

Tenth Annual
Computer Press
Awards ≥1994

WINNER

Eleventh Annual
Computer Press
Awards ≥1995

IDG is the world's leading IT media, research and exposition company. Founded in 1964, IDG had 1997 revenues of $2.05 billion and has more than 9,000 employees worldwide. IDG offers the widest range of media options that reach IT buyers in 75 countries representing 95% of worldwide IT spending. IDG's diverse product and services portfolio spans six key areas including print publishing, online publishing, expositions and conferences, market research, education and training, and global marketing services. More than 90 million people read one or more of IDG's 290 magazines and newspapers, including IDG's leading global brands — Computerworld, PC World, Network World, Macworld and the Channel World family of publications. IDG Books Worldwide is one of the fastest-growing computer book publishers in the world, with more than 700 titles in 36 languages. The "...For Dummies®" series alone has more than 50 million copies in print. IDG offers online users the largest network of technology-specific Web sites around the world through IDG.net (http://www.idg.net), which comprises more than 225 targeted Web sites in 55 countries worldwide. International Data Corporation (IDC) is the world's largest provider of information technology data, analysis and consulting, with research centers in over 41 countries and more than 400 research analysts worldwide. IDG World Expo is a leading producer of more than 168 globally branded conferences and expositions in 35 countries including E3 (Electronic Entertainment Expo), Macworld Expo, ComNet, Windows World Expo, ICE (Internet Commerce Expo), Agenda, DEMO, and Spotlight. IDG's training subsidiary, ExecuTrain, is the world's largest computer training company, with more than 230 locations worldwide and 785 training courses. IDG Marketing Services helps industry-leading IT companies build international brand recognition by developing global integrated marketing programs via IDG's print, online and exposition products worldwide. Further information about the company can be found at www.idg.com.   1/24/99

Publisher's Acknowledgments

We're proud of this book; please register your comments through our IDG Books Worldwide Online Registration Form located at http://my2cents.dummies.com.

Some of the people who helped bring this book to market include the following:

Acquisitions, Editorial, and Media Development

Project Editor: Rebecca Whitney

Acquisitions Editor: Steve Hayes

Technical Editor: Bill Karow

Editorial Manager: Mary C. Corder

Media Development Manager: Heather Heath Dismore

Production

Project Coordinator: Emily Perkins

Layout and Graphics: Jill Piscitelli, Brent Savage, Michael A. Sullivan, Brian Torwelle, Erin Zeltner

Proofreaders: Laura Albert, Corey Bowen, John Greenough, Arielle Carole Mennelle, Charles Spencer

Indexer: Liz Cunningham

Special Help
Constance C. Carlisle

General and Administrative

IDG Books Worldwide, Inc.: John Kilcullen, CEO; Steven Berkowitz, President and Publisher

IDG Books Technology Publishing Group: Richard Swadley, Senior Vice President and Publisher; Walter Bruce III, Vice President and Associate Publisher; Joseph Wikert, Associate Publisher; Mary Bednarek, Branded Product Development Director; Mary Corder, Editorial Director; Barry Pruett, Publishing Manager; Michelle Baxter, Publishing Manager

IDG Books Consumer Publishing Group: Roland Elgey, Senior Vice President and Publisher; Kathleen A. Welton, Vice President and Publisher; Kevin Thornton, Acquisitions Manager; Kristin A. Cocks, Editorial Director

IDG Books Internet Publishing Group: Brenda McLaughlin, Senior Vice President and Publisher; Diane Graves Steele, Vice President and Associate Publisher; Sofia Marchant, Online Marketing Manager

IDG Books Production for Dummies Press: Debbie Stailey, Associate Director of Production; Cindy L. Phipps, Manager of Project Coordination, Production Proofreading, and Indexing; Tony Augsburger, Manager of Prepress, Reprints, and Systems; Laura Carpenter, Production Control Manager; Shelley Lea, Supervisor of Graphics and Design; Debbie J. Gates, Production Systems Specialist; Robert Springer, Supervisor of Proofreading; Kathie Schutte, Production Supervisor

Dummies Packaging and Book Design: Patty Page, Manager, Promotions Marketing

◆

The publisher would like to give special thanks to Patrick J. McGovern, without whom this book would not have been possible.

◆

Contents at a Glance

Intro: How to Use This Book..1

Part I: Getting to Know the Internet 5

Part II: Getting Started 9

Part III: Electronic Mail 25

Part IV: Usenet Newsgroups...59

Part V: Mailing Lists 71

Part VI: The World Wide Web 79

Part VII: Finding and Using Resources on the Internet 101

Part VIII: Live Online Communication 123

Part IX: Advanced Topics 149

Part X: Classic Internet..169

Appendix: Internet Country Codes 175

Glossary: Techie Talk 181

Index 197

Book Registration Information ....Back of Book

Table of Contents

Intro: How to Use This Book 1

Finding Things in This Book..2
The Cast of Icons 3
Conventions Used in This Book.......................................3
Where Did That Web Site Go? 4
Feedback, Please 4

Part I: Getting to Know the Internet 5

What Is the Internet? 6
What's So Great about the Internet? 6
What Services Does the Internet Provide?.......................8
Will the Internet Take a Bunch of Your Time? 8

Part II: Getting Started 9

Hooking Up to the Internet First Class 10
    Cable TV...10
    Digital Subscriber Lines (DSL) 11
    Direct connection 12
    ISDN 12
Hooking Up to the Internet Economy 12
    Free e-mail and Internet access services 13
    Libraries and cybercafés 13
    Network computers 13
    Secondhand computers..14
    Set-top boxes...14
Hooking Up to the Internet Coach...................................14
Investing in a Computer for Internet Access 15
    Macintosh — and the iMac — versus Windows 15
    Desktop versus laptop..15
    Is Linux for you? 15
    This year's model versus last year's model 16
    "Free" computers 16
    Making sure that your computer is cable ready 16
    Memory, hard disk, monitor, and printer 16
    Prepare to back up 16
    Upgrading versus buying 17
Modems..17
    Modem specs 17
    Modem types...18
    "What do the lights on my modem mean?" 19
    Other modem tips 20
    Telephone line tips 20

Selecting an Internet Service Provider 21
   Online services 21
   Internet Service Providers (ISPs) 21
   PPP and shell accounts 22
Software for Internet Access 23
   Connection software 23
   Other software 24

Part III: Electronic Mail *25*

Abbreviations and Acronyms 26
ABCs of E-Mail 26
   Electronic etiquette 27
   E-mail caveats 27
   Finding e-mail addresses 29
   Free e-mail 30
   Headers 31
   Rejected mail (bounces) 31
Addresses 32
   "What's my address?" 32
   Host names and domain names 33
   IP addresses and DNS 34
   Top-level domains 34
   Port numbers 36
   URLs versus e-mail addresses 36
America Online and CompuServe Addresses 36
Attachments 37
Smileys and Emoticons 37
Using America Online (AOL) 38
   Finding an address 38
   Reading incoming mail..39
   Sending new mail 39
   Replying to messages...41
   Forwarding messages 41
   Saving messages 41
Using Eudora (Windows and Mac) 41
   Configuring Eudora 42
   Getting incoming mail 42
   Reading incoming mail..43
   Sending new mail 43
   Replying to messages...43
   Forwarding messages 44
   Saving messages 44
   Reading saved messages 44
   Attaching a file 44

Using Juno (Windows) 45
  Getting and installing Juno Software 45
  Reading incoming mail...46
  Composing and sending new mail 46
  Replying to messages...47
  Forwarding messages 48
  Using the address book 48
  Saving messages in a folder 49
Using Netscape Messenger (Windows,
  Mac, Linux, and UNIX) 49
  Setting up Netscape for e-mail 49
  Getting and reading incoming mail 50
  Sending new mail 51
  Replying to messages...52
  Forwarding messages 52
  Saving messages in folders 53
  Reading saved messages 53
Using Outlook Express (Windows and Mac)..................53
  Getting and reading incoming mail 53
  Sending new mail 55
  Replying to messages...55
  Forwarding messages 56
  Saving messages in folders 56
Using Pine (Linux and UNIX) 56
  Running Pine 56
  Reading incoming mail...57
  Sending new mail 57
  Replying to messages...58
  Forwarding messages 58
  Saving messages to a file 58

Part IV: Usenet Newsgroups 59
Deja.com and Usenet Indexers 60
Frequently Asked Questions (FAQs) 61
Newsgroup Names...61
Newsgroup Netiquette 63
Posting Your First Article 64
Ramping Up Your Own Newsgroup.................................65
Reading Newsgroups with America Online 66
Reading Newsgroups with Deja.com................................67
  Searching Deja.com 67
  Using Deja.com as a newsreader 68
  Replying to articles 68
  Posting a new article 69
Reading Newsgroups with Netscape Newsgroup 69
Reading Newsgroups with Outlook Express 70
Reading Newsgroups with Other Newsreader Programs............70

Part V: Mailing Lists 71

Addresses Used with Mailing Lists 72
Finding a Mailing List 73
Getting On and Off a Mailing List...73
    Lists maintained manually 73
    Lists maintained automatically 73
    Web-based lists 74
Open and Closed Mailing Lists 75
Receiving Digested Mailing Lists 75
Sending Messages to a Mailing List..75
Special Requests to Mailing Lists 76
Starting Your Own Mailing List 77
Using Filters 78

Part VI: The World Wide Web........................79

ABCs of the Web..80
Finding Your Way around the Web 81
Kids, Porn, and the Web 82
    Access supervision 83
    Buying filtering software 83
    Using an online service with built-in filtering..............................83
Plug-Ins, Helper Programs, and ActiveX Controls.............................84
    ZipMagic (Windows only)..85
    WinZip (Windows only) 85
    StuffIt Expander and DropStuff with Expander Enhancer
        (Macintosh) 85
    RealPlayer (formerly RealAudio) 85
    Acrobat Reader 86
    Macromedia Shockwave 86
    Apple QuickTime 86
Privacy, Security, and Cookies 86
    Cookies...86
    Secure surfing 87
Problems and Error Messages 88
    Displaying a page takes too long 88
    Error message "The server does not have a DNS entry" 89
    Error message "www.bigsite.com has refused your
        connection" or "Broken pipe" 89
    Error message "404 File Not Found" 89
    Your browser keeps crashing 91
Uniform Resource Locators (URLs) 91
Using AOL to Browse the Web 92
    Viewing a Web page 93
    Changing your home page...93
    Following a hypertext link...94
    Using bookmarks 94

Using Internet Explorer to Browse the Web..................................95
    Viewing a Web page 95
    Changing your home page...95
    Following a hypertext link..96
    Playing favorites 96
    Go for history 97
Using Lynx to Browse the Web 97
    Starting Lynx...97
    Browsing with Lynx 97
Using Netscape Navigator to Browse the Web 98
    Viewing a Web page 99
    Changing your home page...99
    Following a hypertext link..99
    Using bookmarks 100
    Remembering where you came from.................................100
    Using Netscape plug-ins 100

Part VII: Finding and Using Resources on the Internet..........................101

Directories, Search Engines, and Portals 102
    Directories...102
    Engines that search 102
    Portals 103
    Directories, search engines, and portals with a twist...........104
    Power searching 104
    Search strategies 105
Excellent Surfing Ideas 106
Free, Free, Free! 107
Information Sources 107
    The CIA's World Factbook 107
    Encyclopædia Britannica 107
    Libraries...107
    Maps 108
    Regional information providers 108
    Satellites..108
    Statistics and other data 108
    World time 109
Magazines and Literature 109
Music Online...109
Newspapers 110
Selling Online 111
Shareware and Freeware Software 111
    c|net Shareware.com...112
    The Ultimate Collection of Winsock Software (TUCOWS)....112
    The Info-Mac Archive..112

Shopping Online from A to Z 112
    Airlines 113
    Books 113
    Condoms 113
    Dolls and other collectibles 114
    Education...114
    Flowers..114
    Groceries 114
    Houses 114
    Internet service providers...114
    Jobs..114
    Love 115
    Macintoshes 115
    Overcoats and boots 115
    Postage..115
    Quesadillas 115
    Stocks and bonds 115
    Tapes and CDs..116
    Used and new cars 116
    Vitamins 116
    Web page design..116
    Xylophones 116
    Yiddish 116
    Zygotes..116
  "Should I Give Out My Credit Card over the Internet?" 117
  Telephone Directories..117
  Uncompressing and Decoding Retrieved Files 117
    .gif 119
    .gz and .z 119
    .hqx...119
    .jpeg and .jpg...119
    .mp3 119
    .mpeg and .mpg..119
    .sit 119
    .tar...120
    .Z 120
    .zip 120
  Viruses...120

Part VIII: Live Online Communication..........123
  Chatting Online 124
    Conversations: They can be hard to follow 125
    Etiquette for chatting...126
    Safe chatting 127
    Smileys, abbreviations, and emoticons................................128
    Weeding out disruptive chatters 129

Chatting on America Online (AOL) 130
    Beginning to chat 130
    Rooms with a view 131
    Choosing a screen name 132
    Filing a complaint 132
    Instant messages 132
    Private rooms 133
    Profiles 134
    Buddy Lists 134
    Making sounds 135
ICQ 135
    Getting ICQ 135
    Making contact 135
    Let's chat 136
    Take a message 137
    Filing a complaint 137
Internet Relay Chat (IRC) 137
    Starting IRC 138
    Picking a server 138
    Issuing IRC commands...139
    IRC channels 140
    Joining a channel 140
    Leaving a channel..141
    Listing available channels 141
    Choosing an IRC nickname 142
    Holding a private conversation 142
    Starting your own channel 143
    Types of channels...143
    Filing a complaint 144
    Getting more info 144
Web-Based Chat 144
MUDs and MOOs 144
    Using MUDs 145
    Finding MUDs 145
    Getting started in MUDs 146
Internet Telephony 146

Part IX: Advanced Topics 149

Encryption and Internet Security 150
    Cryptography 150
    Public-key cryptography..150
    The politics of cryptography 151
    How secure is public-key cryptography? 151
    Key size 152
    Internet Explorer and Netscape Communicator 152
    Outlook Express and Netscape Messenger 153
    Pretty Good Privacy..153
    Obtaining a copy of PGP 154

Getting started with PGP 155
HushMail 156
Public-key infrastructure..156
Passwords and pass phrases 157
Java and Network Computers 157
Java applets..158
Network computers 158
Internet Radio and TV...159
Creating Your Own Web Home Page 159
Why would you want your own home page? 160
Building your page 160
Tips for effective Web pages...162
Web page maintenance 163
HTML editors 164
Creating a home page on America Online.............................165
Publicizing your page..165
Link exchanges and Webrings 166
META tags 166
Starting a Business on the Web 167

Part X: Classic Internet *169*

FTP 170
Using FTP programs..170
Navigating files and directories 170
Uploading and downloading files...171
Telnet...171
Using telnet from a Winsock or MacTCP program 171
Connecting to remote computers 172
Disconnecting from remote computers 172
UNIX and Linux commands..172
Finger...173

Appendix: Internet Country Codes................*175*

Glossary: Techie Talk *181*

Index *197*

Book Registration Information ......*Back of Book*

How to Use This Book

At last — an Internet reference book that includes all the tasks and resources you really need, lies flat on your desk so that you can type with both hands, and weighs less than a laptop computer! In this book, you will find information about lots of Internet services and how to use them. We have left out the tons of subjects that will have changed completely by the time this book is printed and that you can easily find for yourself, after you know your way around the Net.

We show you how to use online services that offer Internet access, including America Online. We also tell you about the two most popular computer programs for accessing the Internet's World Wide Web: Netscape Communicator and Microsoft Internet Explorer.

The Internet is an active medium. You can't just sit and watch it like television; you have to try things, poke around, and find the sites, information, and people that you need and enjoy. This book will get you started and help you on the way. Welcome aboard and have fun!

Finding Things in This Book

This book is divided into 10 parts (well, 11 with the appendix) so that you can find things by topic. Topics within each part are generally in alphabetical order. The table of contents, Techie Talk glossary, and extensive index should also help you find whatever you need.

Part I, "Getting to Know the Internet," explains what the Internet is and why it may be the most important technological development of the 21st century.

Part II, "Getting Started," tells you just about everything you need to know to get on the Internet. A special section is addressed to people who don't have a great deal of money to spend.

Part III, "Electronic Mail," demystifies the basics of e-mail and describes many popular mailing programs, including Eudora, Netscape, and Outlook Express. This part also has a list of common abbreviations and some tips for "netiquette."

Part IV, "Usenet Newsgroups," introduces you to *Usenet,* a worldwide information system in which you can read messages about thousands of different topics every day, and Deja.com, a Web site that tries to tame Usenet.

Part V, "Mailing Lists," presents another popular source of information, one you can use even if you have only e-mail service. We guide you in finding, getting on, and getting off electronic mailing lists found on the Internet.

Part VI, "The World Wide Web," gets you started in using the service that has propelled the Internet into the spotlight. It decodes the mysteries of hypertext and URLs and tells you how to use some popular Web browsing programs, including Microsoft Internet Explorer and Netscape Navigator.

Part VII, "Finding and Using Resources on the Internet," shows you how to use popular Internet search sites, such as Yahoo! and AltaVista, for finding information about almost any conceivable topic. We even tell you how to find lost friends, download free music and do a little shopping.

Part VIII, "Live Online Communication," helps you use the Internet to meet people and hold live conversations with them by using the chat facilities of AOL, ICQ, Internet Relay Chat (IRC), and MUDs. *Warning:* Reading this part can be hazardous to your free time.

Part IX, "Advanced Topics," briefs you on hot subjects such as Internet security, encryption, the PGP program, building your own Web home page, Internet telephone, Java, network computers, and starting an online business.

Part X, "Classic Internet," tells you about some Internet tools from days long ago, before all-purpose Web browsers came on the scene. These tools, still used on the Web, include telnet and ftp. We also give you a quick guide to UNIX commands.

The appendix, "Internet Country Codes," lists all the two-letter codes that tell you which countries your international e-mail messages come from.

The extensive glossary at the end of this book explains in plain English the baffling jargon you encounter on the Internet.

Finally, we include a comprehensive index to help you find what you are looking for.

The Cast of Icons

For each resource or task we describe — and whenever we provide other important information — we include icons that tell you about what you are reading.

We give you a tip that can save you time or keep you from looking like a newcomer on the Internet.

Watch out! We learned about this information the hard way.

Who knows why, but this resource or task may not work as you might expect.

This icon points to the speediest way to do something.

Follow this handy cross-reference to other related *...For Dummies* books that cover this topic in more detail.

Conventions Used in This Book

Text that you may need to type into your computer appears in `this typeface`. Short commands appear in boldface, like this: Type **telnet.** When you have to enter information that's specific to your own situation, just that part is shown in italics: *username*@`aol.com`, for example.

Throughout the book, you will see strange-looking things like `http://net.gurus.com`. These mysterious snippets of text are

Uniform Resource Locators, or *URLs.* They tell your computer where to find things on the Internet. We explain URLs in detail in the section "Uniform Resource Locators (URLs)," in Part VI.

Be sure to type input text just as it appears in this book. Use the same capitalization as we do, because some computers on the Internet consider the capitalized and small versions of the same letter to be totally different beasts.

However, when a URL or e-mail address appears at the end of a sentence — here and in other publications — the rules of English demand that a period follow. It's almost never part of the address. Remember not to type that final period when you enter that URL or address into your computer.

URLs can be long and sometimes go over to the next line. Some publications add a hyphen at that point, if one wasn't there already. If you see a hyphen in a URL at a line break, type the hyphen. If the URL doesn't work, try it without that hyphen.

Where Did That Web Site Go?

The Internet is constantly changing, so some of the links and resources we have painstakingly selected may disappear by the time you read this book. Look at the Web page for this book for corrections and updates. Go to http://net.gurus.com and follow the All Books link to find the pages about this book. *See also* "Problems and Error Messages," in Part VI, for other tips on following missing links.

Feedback, Please

We love getting feedback about this book. Please write to us at idq6@gurus.com. You get a friendly message back from our mailbot, although we humans read it too. We have updates to the book, too, at our Web site, at net.gurus.com.

For information about other books in this series, visit the official *...For Dummies* Web site, at www.dummies.com, or send e-mail to info@dummies.com.

Part 1

Getting to Know the Internet

Big as it is, the Internet is still in its early stages. Destined to become the primary means of communication and commerce in the 21st century, the Net now resembles a new city, filled with magnificent architecture and empty facades, broad boulevards and dirt roads, sumptuous plazas and muddy lots. Swarms of people are already working there, some in carefully planned facilities and others in makeshift shacks. The smell of success and big money is in the air. Tycoons and bankers are wandering around making big bets while politicians and bureaucrats keep trying to establish control, without success. Reporters comb the back alleys for stories about its dark side. Even though the Net is only half built and the architects are continually revising the plans, its diverse neighborhoods are throbbing with energy.

In this part . . .

✔ **What is the Internet, anyway?**

✔ **What can you do with it?**

✔ **Why should you bother?**

What Is the Internet?

The *Internet* is a system that lets computers all over the world talk to each other. That's all you really need to know. If you have access to a computer, you can probably use "the Net."

The U.S. Department of Defense Advanced Research Projects Agency originally sponsored Internet development because it wanted a military communications system that could survive a nuclear war. Later, the Internet was funded as a research support system by the National Science Foundation. That's all ancient history now, though, because support for the Internet comes almost entirely from commercial sources.

Today, an Internet Society tries to make policy, and an Internet Engineering Task Force sets standards with considerable aplomb. The White House is trying to establish an international Internet organization, although at the moment no one is in charge. The Internet is anarchy at its best and worst.

What's So Great about the Internet?

What makes the Internet great is that it brings together the best qualities of the communications systems that preceded it while improving on their worst features:

+ **Postal mail (known as *snail mail* on the Net):** Takes at least a day — often a week — to get to its destination, and you must have envelopes, buy stamps, go to a mailbox, and so on. If you are away from home, your mail piles up unanswered. E-mail is quicker to compose, arrives faster, and doesn't require a stamp.

+ **The telephone:** The other person must be available to talk, and usually no record exists of what was said. You can read e-mail when you feel like it, and it doesn't interrupt you during dinner.

+ **The fax machine:** It's a chore to incorporate a fax in another document or to pass it on to someone else. Faxes of faxes of faxes become illegible. E-mail stays readable no matter how many times it's forwarded.

+ **The public library:** You have to go to the library to find information, and half the time the book you want is checked out or missing. By the time information gets into the library, it is often out of date. The Internet is open 24 hours a day, seven days a week, and you don't have to get in your car to go there.

✦ **The newspaper:** Most newspapers come out only once a day, and they decide what news you get to see and what spin to put on it. On the World Wide Web, news is updated continuously. (On the other hand, it's hard to line a litter box with a Web page.)

Other qualities that make the Internet so compelling to "surf":

✦ Its democratic nature

✦ Its capability to let people communicate, even if they are never at their computers at the same time

✦ Its basis in text, getting people to communicate in writing again

✦ Its relatively low cost to use

✦ Its lack of geographic boundaries

✦ Its capacity to bring together people with similar interests

✦ Its offer of instant gratification

The Internet is also full of contradictions:

✦ It is amazingly fast, yet it often feels agonizingly slow.

✦ It is held together by chewing gum and baling wire, yet it survives manmade and natural disasters when other communications systems fail. (Remember why it was invented?)

✦ It is scandalously vulnerable to hackers, yet it hosts an encryption system, PGP, that is almost the only truly secure means of communications available to the general public. (***See also*** Part IX.)

✦ Its content is often sophomoric, yet powerful corporations and governments fear it and seek to rein it in.

✦ Its day-to-day operation depends on the cooperation of thousands of computers and their human administrators, yet it lacks any central control, operating almost entirely by consensus and social pressure.

No one really knows what the Net will be like in ten years, although one thing is for sure: We won't think of it as a single "thing." Different parts of the Net have already developed their own characteristics. No one knows all its intricacies, any more than anyone can know all the regions of a large country or all the neighborhoods of a great city.

What Services Does the Internet Provide?

The Internet provides these basic services:

✦ Electronic mail, or e-mail (*see also* Part III)

✦ Access to the World Wide Web, or just the Web — the information system of the 21st century (*see also* Part VI)

✦ Newsgroups (*see also* Part IV)

✦ Mailing lists (*see also* Part V)

✦ File transfers from other computers (*see also* Part VII)

✦ The capability to log on to other computers (*see also* Part IX)

✦ Discussions with other people using chat (*see also* Part VIII)

Advanced services under development include multimedia broadcasts, Internet radio, secure transactions, video conferencing, and wireless communication.

You can do an almost endless list of things with the Internet, from finding a job to finding a mate, from searching the card catalogs of the greatest libraries in the world to ordering a pizza. Most important, the Internet is the place to learn more about the Internet. We tell you in Part II how to get on the Internet. Have fun!

Will the Internet Take a Bunch of Your Time?

Not necessarily. Reading your e-mail and catching up on a favorite mailing list can take just 15 minutes per day. But beware: The Internet can be addictive! You don't have enough hours in a day to keep up with all of it.

People who spend too much time surfing the Net are often told, "Get a life!" On the other hand, a recent survey shows that the average American spends, on a weekly basis, 2.6 hours a day watching television and videos. Watching the tube ranks third only to sleeping (7.2 hours) and working (3.1 hours). Other surveys show that when people start using the Net, they spend less time watching TV.

So, you couch potatoes out there: Turn off the TV and log on! It's happening big-time on the Internet.

Part II

Getting Started

Getting on the Internet is much easier than it used to be. The process still can be daunting to new users, however. We try to help you as you figure out the world of modems, Internet Service Providers, and communications software you may need in order to connect to the Net. It used to be that either your computer had a direct connection to the Internet at school or work or you bought a modem and dialed in over an ordinary phone line. Today, you have many more choices, including cable, radio, and specialized telephone services like DSL and ISDN — and you don't even need a computer. To help you make sense out of all these choices, we've organized your Internet connection options into three groups: first class, economy, and coach.

In this part . . .

✔ How to hook up to the Internet

✔ How to buy a computer for Internet access

✔ How to select a modem

✔ How to select an Internet Service Provider

✔ What software you need to use the Internet

Hooking Up to the Internet First Class

First class is the Internet the way it was meant to be — *fast.* If you use an ordinary phone line to access the Internet and then switch to first-class service, you never want to switch back. Here's how you get it.

Cable TV

The friendly people who sell you cable TV service are, or soon will be, selling Internet access also. Your Internet data travels over the same coaxial cable that brings you *Oprah, ER,* and *Seinfeld* reruns. That cable can move your data as much as 25 times faster than conventional telephone modems. If cable Internet service is available in your area, if your computer can support it, and if you can afford it, it's worth the higher price. The improvement it makes is the difference between watching previews of coming attractions and seeing the real movie. Here's what you need to know about cable:

+ Cable Internet service is rated at 1.5 million bits per second. By comparison, conventional phone modems offer up to 56,000 bits per second, and ISDN offers 128,000 bits per second. DSL is about as fast as cable.

+ Your computer shares a high-speed party line with several other computers in your neighborhood. As the cable company signs up more subscribers, your computer's performance may go down somewhat during peak periods.

+ The most modern cable modems are two-way and run your entire Internet connection via the cable. Older systems are one-way, receiving data via cable but still using a regular dial-up modem and phone line to send data.

+ Data congestion can still occur in other places on the Internet, particularly during peak times of the day or when a major event, such as a natural disaster or stock market crash, occurs.

+ The monthly cost is two to three times the cost of conventional telephone Internet access. You may get a discount if you already have cable TV service.

+ You don't have to buy a modem; your cable company can rent you one as part of the package. It can also sell you a network interface card if your computer doesn't have an Ethernet port.

+ The cable company installs the necessary hardware and software and gets you up and running. You may have to take half a day off for the installation.

+ Be sure to back up your computer's hard disk before your installation appointment. Many cable installers have limited computer experience.

✦ Two-way cable Internet access doesn't tie up your phone line. If you have a second phone line for your computer, deduct its cost from the cable company's monthly charges when you're deciding whether you can afford cable.

✦ With 2-way cable modems, you're always online. You never have to dial in.

✦ Many cable companies restrict you to personal use unless you buy a more expensive commercial-access package.

✦ Cable Internet access doesn't interfere with your cable TV reception.

✦ Your cable company is also your Internet Service Provider (ISP). As monopolies, cable television companies do not have a great reputation for service.

✦ America Online (AOL) has a Bring Your Own Access plan that lets cable Internet subscribers take advantage of the AOL value-added services at a reduced price. Go to keyword **byoa**.

✦ You normally leave your cable modem on all the time. The cable modem may take 15 minutes or so after a power failure to resynchronize itself with the cable company's network.

✦ If you travel with a laptop, ask your cable company whether it has a phone number you can dial to get your e-mail.

Digital Subscriber Lines (DSL)

DSL is a family of technologies, including ADSL, that enable phone companies to offer Internet access over phone wires at a speed comparable to cable modems. DSL gives cable companies some meaningful competition. The people we know who have it think that it's great. Unfortunately, not all phone companies offer it now, although many more will introduce it in the near future.

✦ With DSL, you're connected all the time and you can still use the phone line for voice calls.

✦ DSL doesn't work if you live too far from the telephone company central office.

✦ Pricing depends on speed, with 640,000 bps the slowest and the cheapest rate.

✦ You may have to pay extra if you don't want your local phone company as your Internet Service Provider.

✦ You need an Ethernet port or interface card.

Some versions of DSL connect to your TV and allow you to watch movies on demand. Also, some cable modems let you make phone calls. Real competition may be coming to a utility pole near you.

Direct connection

If you're at a university or work for a large corporation, you can probably get connected to the Internet directly by using the organization's computer network. You don't need a modem or phone line, although you may need a network interface card. In almost every organization that provides direct connections, a person is available who can help you get started. Ask to see the system administrator — and bring cookies.

ISDN

ISDN, which stands for Integrated Services Digital Network, can operate at two to three times the speed of a 56,000 bps modem. ISDN should work with your existing phone wiring. Some phone companies promote ISDN, and others make you drag it out of them. Some, schizophrenically, do both.

ISDN is still expensive in many places, and installing it can be complicated. If cable or DSL is available in your area or will be soon, they are better choices. If not, ISDN may be your only option to get first-class service. Here are some hints:

+ For ISDN, you need an ISDN terminal adapter, or TA (think of it as an ISDN modem). Buy one that your phone company recommends.

+ Like modems, terminal adapters can be internal or external. Make sure that the TA comes with a regular phone jack on it so that you can plug in a normal telephone for voice calls.

+ Phone companies offer dozens of ISDN options, including Caller ID and 3-way calling. Buy only what you need.

+ Windows 98 comes with ISDN support. Choose Start⇨ Programs⇨Accessories⇨Communications⇨ISDN Configuration Wizard).

If you want to try ISDN, get a copy of *ISDN For Dummies,* 2nd Edition, by David Angell (IDG Books Worldwide, Inc.).

Hooking Up to the Internet Economy

If you want to surf the Internet and you have a tight budget, you have many more options than you used to have.

Free e-mail and Internet access services

Several companies offer free Internet access in return for showing you ads. Although these free services are perfect for nonprofit organizations or anyone with a tight budget, don't expect much support:

✦ **Juno:** If you have a Windows computer but cannot afford monthly Internet access fees, Juno gives you an e-mail account for free. You see advertisements when you check your mail. *See also* Part III for more details about Juno and free e-mail.

✦ **NetZero:** NetZero offers free, advertising-supported Internet and e-mail access for Windows 95, Windows 98, and Windows NT users. A Macintosh version is planned. To request a CD-ROM containing the necessary software, phone (888) 279-8132. You pay a small charge for shipping and handling.

✦ **AltaVista:** AltaVista also offers free Internet access to Windows users. You have to download a small program that can fit on a floppy disk, so you first need to get access through a friend or library. Visit `microav.com` for more information.

✦ **Freeserve:** In the United Kingdom, Freeserve offers free Internet access and has local phone numbers. Go to `www.freeserve.net` for details. (Note that Freeserve uses some *proxy server* settings that other ISPs do not, so consult someone there before installing Internet connection software if you have a Freeserve account.)

For other service, start at Yahoo (`www.yahoo.com`) and choose Business and Economy, Companies, Internet Services, Access Providers, and Free Internet Access.

Many free services analyze what you do online to target to your interests the ads they display.

Libraries and cybercafés

You don't have to spend any money to use the Internet. Many local libraries now have public Internet-access machines. With free e-mail services, you can have your own, private Internet address. *See also* Part III.

You can also visit a *cybercafé* — a coffee bar that rents time on online computers. You may meet some people there who can help you with whatever problems you encounter.

Network computers

Network computers don't have hard disks. All the software and data you use is downloaded over a computer network. Although some people think that network computers will displace personal computers in many applications, network computers won't be suitable for personal use for a while. Others think that network computers are a bad idea that has already failed twice. Don't be the first on your block to get one.

Secondhand computers

The steady decline in the price of new computers has pushed the price of used machines to very affordable levels. However, if you know nothing about computers and have no desire to find out and no one knowledgeable to assist you, you may be better off with a low-end new computer or a set-top box.

Set-top boxes

One new option for connection to the Internet is the set-top box. As its name implies, it's a box the size of a small VCR that sits on top of your television set. (The best-known brand is called WebTV, from Microsoft.) You hook it up to your TV in much the same way as you hook up a VCR, and you also plug the set-top box into a telephone jack. *Voilà!* You're connected to the Internet — without a computer. These units are available for as little as $100 plus $20 per month for Internet service. Although set-top boxes do work, they have some drawbacks:

✦ Because televisions can display only a half-dozen or so lines of text at a time, you tediously have to press Page Down repeatedly to read even a modest-size Internet page.

✦ You're usually limited to one Internet Service Provider. The monthly rate is about the same as for regular Internet service.

✦ You cannot use set-top boxes for much more than looking at World Wide Web pages (*see also* Part VI), text chat, and e-mail.

On the other hand, set-top boxes cost much less than a computer, and fewer things can go wrong. If you do buy one, we strongly recommend getting the optional keyboard too.

Hooking Up to the Internet Coach

Most people fly coach, and most users access the Internet over an ordinary phone line. You need

✦ A computer

✦ A modem

✦ A phone line

✦ An Internet Service Provider (ISP)

✦ Software for Internet access

Most new computers come with built-in modems and Internet access software already installed.

We tell you more about these options in the following section.

Investing in a Computer for Internet Access

If you aren't using an Internet appliance, such as a set-top box, you need a computer. Almost any new computer you can buy today is ready for Internet use. Although computer salespeople will try to sell you the most expensive model possible, here's what you really need to get on the Internet.

Macintosh — and the iMac — versus Windows

Which type of computer to buy is a "religious" decision. Apple fanatics tout the clean design and ease of use of the Macintosh software. Microsoft users point out that they're in the majority and claim that Windows 95 and Windows 98 make a PC almost as good as a Mac. Both work fine.

Apple's new Internet-ready iMac and iBook come in spiffy packages with a built-in color display screen and are very easy to set up. Here are some things you should know about the iMac and iBook:

✦ Both have built-in modems and Ethernet ports, so they're ready for cable and DSL modems.

✦ Neither has a floppy disk, although you can buy one as an option or just use the Internet to transfer files.

✦ The new iMac DV connects directly to digital camcorders and lets you edit your home movies and put your work on the Internet in QuickTime format.

Desktop versus laptop

Although laptops are really cool, they cost much more for the same performance. Get a desktop model unless you plan to travel frequently with your computer.

Is Linux for you?

Linux is a free version of the UNIX operating system. It supports a full range of tools for Internet access and has a very loyal following. Indeed, many ISPs use Linux on their servers. Although Linux is very powerful, it is still complex to install and use. We think that beginners should stick to Macs and Windows.

This year's model versus last year's model

Computer manufacturers come out with new models every year or so. You can save as much as $1,000 by buying last year's model. These days, either model is fine for Internet use. If you can afford it, go for the newest model available. If you're tight, take the bargain.

"Free" computers

Some companies are offering computers for free. There's a catch, however: You're required to sign up for several years of pricey Internet service. If you aren't happy with their service, if prices drop, or if you decide a year from now to switch to cable or DSL, too bad.

Making sure that your computer is cable ready

Make sure that any computer you buy can be used with a cable or DSL modem — some new PCs that sell for less than $600 cannot! To be cable ready, your computer must have either something called an Ethernet port or an available slot into which you can plug an Ethernet card. The slot may be called a PCI, ISA, NuBus, or PCcard slot — just make sure that any computer you buy has one.

Memory, hard disk, monitor, and printer

An adequate amount of memory (RAM) does more for your computer's performance than processor speed. These days, 32MB of RAM is the minimum. Get 64MB or more if you can afford it.

Most new desktop machines have at least 2 gigabytes (GB) of hard disk space, more than enough for Internet use.

The basic color monitor that comes with most computers these days will do for Internet use. Step up one level if you feel rich. Anything beyond that level is overkill for the Net.

Almost all modern printers can print graphics. Any printer will do. You can even live without a printer while you're getting started, although having one is handy.

Prepare to back up

Hard disks are much more reliable these days, although they still crash sometimes. And they're just too big to back up to floppy disks. A removable cartridge tape or disk drive is cheap insurance against data loss. Remember to back up regularly or else you'll be sorry that you didn't.

Some companies back up your computer automatically over the Internet — for a fee, of course. You can find a list of such companies at Yahoo (www.yahoo.com): Choose Business and Economy, Companies, Computers, Services, and Backup.

Upgrading versus buying

If your computer is more than two years old, it probably isn't worth upgrading. If you can afford to buy a new one, do so. Otherwise, save your quarters and wait. If you choose to upgrade, just get a bigger hard disk or add more memory (RAM). Processor upgrades are rarely worth the trouble.

For lots of information, check out a copy of *Upgrading and Fixing PCs,* 3rd Edition, by Andy Rathbone (IDG Books Worldwide, Inc.).

What should you do with your old computer? Give it to a charitable institution and take a tax deduction. Your kids will sneer at an obsolete machine, and selling it is a hassle. Call your local school district, library, church, synagogue, mosque, or other charity and offer the computer as a donation, or visit `www.microweb.com/ pepsite/Recycle/recycle_index.html`, which lists computer recyclers by state and country.

Be sure to get a written receipt that details everything you donated, including software. Tax laws are changing, so get up-to-date advice about how much you can deduct.

Modems

If you're connecting to the Internet by using an ordinary phone line, your modem is a key link. Most new computers come with modems built in. Most conventional modems sold today support speeds as high as 56,000 bits per second (bps). This speed is about the best you can do in a 2-way modem using ordinary phone service.

Modem specs

Modem speeds are specified in *bits per second (bps).* A *kilobit per second,* or *Kbps,* is a thousand bps. A *megabit per second (Mbps)* is a million bps. Sometimes, people (incorrectly) say "baud" rather than "bits per second." Higher is better.

When you're choosing a modem, call your Internet Service Provider or online service and ask the customer-service folks which brand of modem they recommend. They talk every day to people with modem trouble and know which modems are reliable.

Get a copy of *Modems For Dummies,* 3rd Edition, by Tina Rathbone (IDG Books Worldwide, Inc.), for more detailed information about modem selection.

Modems are also rated by the fastest ITU-T (International Telecommunications Union) standard the modem can keep up with. These standards are called *V-dot* numbers because the standards look like V.nn, where *nn* is a number. Sometimes, the name ends with *bis,* which is "and a half" in French. Although higher numbers are generally faster, note that V.42 has nothing to do with speed. Here's a table of modem-specification gobbledygook:

Name	Speed	Comment
Cable	1,400 Kbps	Your cable TV company provides this service.
CDPD	9.6 Kbps radio modem	Works with cell phone technology.
DSL	640 Kbps and higher	Requires special phone service.
V.32bis can	14.4 Kbps	Early 1990s technology. Okay if you get one for free.
V.34	28.8 Kbps	Useable.
V.34bis	33.6 Kbps	Last year's model. Buy one new if you're on a tight budget.
V.42, V.42bis	N/A	Relates to error correction and MNP-5 compression standards. Most new modems support them. Nice to have, but unrelated to modem speed.
V.90	56 Kbps	Full speed on download from V.90-equipped service providers only; otherwise, 33,600 bps. Replaces x2 and K56flex.
x2	56 Kbps	USRobotics technology. Replaced by V.90.
K56flex	56 Kbps	Rockwell technology. Replaced by V.90

Modem types

Modems come in various shapes and sizes. Yours fits in one of the following categories:

✦ **External:** This type of modem is a box or other shape roughly the size of a small book; it connects to a serial port on your computer.

✦ **Internal:** This type of modem is a card that plugs in to a slot inside your computer; internal modems work with only the model of computer for which they're made.

✦ **PC Card or PCMCIA:** These little units look like fat credit cards; they're used mostly in laptop computers. Watch out: The cable that goes to your phone jack can be a little flimsy.

✦ **Cable:** The unit connects to your cable TV jack rather than to your phone line.

✦ **Radio:** These units connect your laptop to a cellular radio service. Although they let you connect to the Internet without a wire, they're pricey and slow. Coverage can be spotty, too.

When you're shopping for a modem, always buy one that's made for your kind of computer.

"What do the lights on my modem mean?"

Here's a list of some common modem lights and what they mean. Your modem's manual should have a complete list.

Label	Name	What It Means
AA	Auto-Answer	The modem may answer the phone.
CD	Carrier Detect	The modem is connected to another computer.
DC	Data Compression	Your modem and the modem to which it's connecting have agreed to use compression.
EC	Error Correction	Your modem and the modem to which it's connecting have agreed to use error correction.
HS	High Speed	Your modem is ready to go at least 4800 bps.
MR	Modem Ready	The power is on.
OH	Off Hook	The modem has "picked up the phone."
RD	Receive Data	Blinks when the modem is receiving data.
SD	Send Data	Blinks when the modem is talking to your computer.
TM	Test Mode	Flashes when you first turn on your modem. Later, it means that your modem has detected an error.
TR	Terminal Ready	Your computer says that it's ready for data.
V.*nn*		Your modem is using the V.*nn* protocol.

Here's a quick guide to interpreting your modem's lights:

✦ If a bunch of lights are on and some are blinking or dim, your modem is hard at work and all is well.

✦ If one or two lights are on steadily, you haven't logged in yet or you have lost your connection.

✦ If none of the lights is on, the switch in back of the modem is off, the modem's power module isn't plugged in, or the modem is broken.

Other modem tips

✦ If someone picks up an extension phone while you're logged in, it may break your connection.

✦ If you have call waiting and a TouchTone phone, type ***70,** (don't forget the comma) in front of the number of your Internet Service Provider in your communications software. This code turns off call waiting while your modem is on the phone. If you have a pulse-dial phone and call waiting, type **1170,** before the phone number.

✦ If you're having problems, it often helps to turn your modem off and then on again and then restart your computer.

✦ If your modem dies, buy a new one. Modems are usually not worth repairing.

Telephone line tips

Your ordinary phone line is all you need to connect to the Internet. If you end up tying up the phone frequently, you may want to get a second line. Here are some other tips:

✦ If your phone company gives you a choice of local service options, pick one that lets you call your Internet Service Provider without per-minute charges.

✦ You need a modular phone jack to plug in your modem. If you don't have one, Radio Shack stores carry a wide line of adapters and wiring stuff. If you're traveling to another country, check to find out what kind of jacks are used there.

✦ If you do get a second line, don't add extensions and don't get call waiting.

✦ Business service costs much more than residential service.

Selecting an Internet Service Provider

Perhaps the most important — and confusing — decision you have to make to get on the Internet is selecting an *Internet Service Provider (ISP).* An ISP connects your computer to the Internet. Some offer additional features to attract your business.

Online services

An *online service* is a company that provides information online, separate from what is available on the Internet. America Online (AOL) is by far the biggest value-added service. Many consider it the best service for beginners. AOL recently acquired CompuServe and promotes that service for business and professional users. Microsoft Network is still trying to become a player. Prodigy has faded. All these online services also provide access to the Internet itself, including sending and receiving Internet e-mail and viewing Web pages.

If you call the major online services, they will send you a free starter kit with the software you need and usually some promotional offer.

Online Service	Phone Number(s)
America Online (AOL)	800-827-6364; 703-448-8700
CompuServe	800-848-8990; 614-718-2800
Microsoft Network (MSN)	800-386-5550

Reasons for picking an online service include a user-friendly interface, special features unique to that provider, and lots of user support.

Although the online services support users well, when something new comes along, months (or even years) may pass before they can offer it. Most of the unique features that online services have typically provided — such as stock quotes, airline reservations, and news magazines — are now available directly on the Internet.

One important exception is online chat (*see also* Part VIII). Most online services allow only their members to participate in the live, online conversations called *chat*. The more members an online service has, the more likely you can find someone interesting to chat with at any given time. The size of America Online gives its chat rooms an overwhelming advantage.

Internet Service Providers (ISPs)

Standard ISPs just connect you to the Internet. They can be big corporations, such as AT&T or Sprint, or they can be run from someone's garage. Bigger is not necessarily better. The most important feature to check about an ISP is that it has an access number that is a local call for you: Otherwise, your phone bill will go through the roof. Other reasons to go with an ISP include

+ Lower cost

+ Higher speeds

+ A choice of access tools (Netscape Navigator, Internet Explorer, or Eudora, for example)

+ The capability to use the latest Internet services as soon as they hit the Net

+ Less censorship

+ Inclusion in your cable or DSL service package

To find an ISP, ask around or check the business pages in your local newspaper. If someone you know has access to the World Wide Web, bug her and go to `thelist.internet.com` for a huge list of providers sorted by state or area code. Consider the following issues when you're picking an ISP:

✦ Flat fee versus hourly charge

✦ System availability during peak periods

✦ Good support, particularly when you're first getting connected and after normal business hours

✦ Space provided for building your own Web pages (**see also** the section in Part IX about creating your own Web home page)

✦ Modem speeds and support for 56 Kbps technology

✦ Arrangements to let you dial in from other locations

✦ For Macintosh users, assurance that your ISP offers wholehearted support for Macintosh Internet applications

It's not unreasonable to try several ISPs before picking the one you like best. Remember, however, that after you start giving out your e-mail address, it's harder to switch ISPs.

PPP and shell accounts

Almost all dial-up ISPs offer *PPP accounts* — accounts that let your computer connect directly to the Internet. You can use all kinds of cool Windows and Mac software, such as Netscape Navigator, Internet Explorer, and Eudora. In case you're curious, PPP stands for Point-to-Point Protocol.

If you have a very old computer or have special access needs, you may prefer a *shell account,* an account that connects your computer to the ISP's computer, usually a UNIX machine. From there, you can hop on the Internet. You're usually restricted to seeing text and can't use new programs, such as Netscape Navigator or Internet Explorer. The Pine e-mail program is popular with shell account users. **See also** "Using Pine," in Part III.

See *UNIX For Dummies,* 4th Edition, by John Levine and Margaret Levine Young (IDG Books Worldwide, Inc.), for more information about how to use UNIX shell accounts.

Software for Internet Access

To connect to and use the Internet, you usually need a program to connect to your account and programs for e-mail, the Web, and other Internet services you want to use.

AOL and CompuServe combine the connection program with e-mail, Web, and other programs — each comes with a free all-in-one program for using its online service.

Connection software

To connect to your Internet account, you need a program to dial the phone and make the connection (if you use AOL, CompuServe, or another online service, use the connection program it provides):

✦ **Windows 98 and 95** come with Dial-Up Networking to connect to dial-up accounts: choose Start⇨Programs⇨Accessories⇨ Communications⇨Dial-Up Networking. Windows 98 and Windows 95 also come with the Internet Connection Wizard, which steps you through the process of setting up a Dial-Up Networking connection.

The Internet Connection Wizard recommends ISPs that have made a deal with Microsoft to appear on its preferred ISP list. This list doesn't necessarily include all ISPs that serve your area. Worse, the ISPs listed may not be a local call from where you are: Be sure to check with your telephone company after you get the access number from the ISP, to confirm that the call is local.

✦ **Macs** come with dial-up software too, called *MacTCP,* and pretty much everything else you'll need. If you have an older Mac, ask your ISP for connection software.

✦ **Windows 3.1 and DOS** don't come with Internet connection software: Ask your ISP which software it can provide. Most ISPs distribute a shareware Windows 3.1 program named Trumpet Winsock.

✦ **Linux** includes a PPP program that can dial in to an ISP account.

Other software

You also need

✦ **A browser:** A *browser* is a program that lets you access the World Wide Web, along with most other types of information on the Net. The two most popular browsers are Netscape Navigator and Communicator and Microsoft Internet Explorer. Both are good products. *See also* Part VI for more detail about browsers.

✦ **An e-mail program:** The Netscape Navigator and Internet Explorer browsers come with e-mail programs (Netscape Messenger and Outlook Express, to be specific). You may want to use a separate program, such as Eudora, that is easier to use and has more features. Part III discusses e-mail programs, and Part IV describes Usenet newsgroups, which you can read using either an e-mail program like Outlook Express or a browser like Netscape.

✦ **Special programs for specialized Internet services:** Browsers don't give you access to all Internet services. You may need other programs to transfer files via FTP or log on to other computers by using telnet (*see also* Part X to find out how these services work). You can also get programs that enable you to participate in online, real-time discussions by using Internet Relay Chat and instant messaging systems (*see also* Part VIII).

We discuss these topics in more detail throughout the rest of this book.

Part III

Electronic Mail

Electronic mail, or e-mail, is without a doubt the most widely used Internet service. Internet mail is connected to most other e-mail systems. After you've mastered Internet e-mail, you can send messages to folks with accounts at most big organizations and educational institutions as well as to folks with accounts at Internet providers and online services. This part of the book describes how to send and receive e-mail, how to figure out what your e-mail address is, how to practice proper e-mail etiquette, and how to use some popular e-mail programs.

In this part . . .

- ✓ **Abbreviations and acronyms**
- ✓ **Addresses**
- ✓ **Attached files**
- ✓ **Etiquette**
- ✓ **Caveats**
- ✓ **Finding e-mail addresses**
- ✓ **Headers**
- ✓ **Sending e-mail to other online services**
- ✓ **Smileys and emoticons**
- ✓ **Using popular e-mail programs, including America Online, Juno, Outlook Express, Netscape Messenger, and Pine**

Abbreviations and Acronyms

EUOA! (E-mail users often abbreviate.) Here are some of the most widely used abbreviations or acronyms:

Acronym	What It Means
AFAIK	As Far As I Know
AKA	Also Known As
BTW	By The Way
FAQ	Frequently Asked Questions (**see also** "Frequently Asked Questions," in Part IV)
FYI	For Your Information
IANAL	I Am Not A Lawyer (but here's my legal advice anyway)
IIRC	If I Recall Correctly
IMHO	In My Humble Opinion
IMNSHO	In My Not-So-Humble Opinion
NRN	No Response Necessary
LOL	Laughing Out Loud
RSN	Real Soon Now (Not!)
ROTFL	Rolling On The Floor, Laughing
RTFM	Read The Manual (you should have looked it up yourself)
TIA	Thanks In Advance
WRT	With Respect To
YMMV	Your Mileage May Vary

For lots more abbreviations and acronyms, check out *Babel: A Glossary of Computer-Oriented Abbreviations and Acronyms* at this URL:

`www.access.digex.net/~ikind/babel.html`

See also "Smileys and Emoticons," later in this part.

ABCs of E-Mail

You need to know a few things to survive in the world of e-mail.

Electronic etiquette

An electronic-mail message can seem rude or obnoxious to the recipient, even when you didn't mean it that way. Here are a few suggestions regarding mail style:

+ Watch your tone. Be especially polite to strangers.

+ Avoid foul language.

+ Don't *flame*. That is, don't send messages full of pointless and excessive outrage. For example:

  ```
  What kind of stupid idiot thinks he can tell
      people how to write their mail?
  ```

+ Double-check your humor — irony and sarcasm are easy to miss. Sometimes, it helps to add a *smiley* to let your reader in on the joke (**see also** "Smileys and Emoticons," later in this part). For example:

  ```
  What kind of stupid idiot thinks he can tell
      people how to write their mail? :-)
  ```

+ If you do get involved in a vitriolic exchange of messages, known on the Net as a *flame war,* the best way to stop is to let the other person have the last word.

+ Your subject line should tell the recipient as much as possible about your message, without getting too long. "Tonight's softball game canceled" is much better than "Important announcement." Don't try to put your entire message on the subject line, though.

+ Check your spelling. Use a word processor to compose your message if your mail program lacks a spell-check feature.

+ Don't send attachments (files) unless you have asked the recipient first. Make sure that the person who will receive the file wants it and has a program that can open it. For example, if you send a PowerPoint presentation to someone who doesn't have Microsoft PowerPoint, the file is useless.

+ When in doubt, save your message overnight. Read and edit it again in the morning before you send it. *Never send e-mail when you are angry or upset!*

E-mail caveats

+ Forging e-mail return addresses is not very hard, so if you get a totally off-the-wall message that seems out of character coming from that person, somebody else may have forged it as a prank.

+ Many people on the Internet adopt fictional personas. The lonely flight attendant you're chatting up may be a 15-year-old boy. "On the Internet, no one knows you're a dog," says a cartoon in the *New Yorker.*

✦ E-mail is not very private. As your mail passes from site to site, it can be read by not only hackers but also your system administrator. Your employer may even have a legal right to read your mail at work. If you really need privacy, *see* "Pretty Good Privacy" and "HushMail," in Part IX.

✦ Injudicious e-mail messages are nearly impossible to erase because they tend to end up on computer backup tapes. *Think about the harm your message may cause in the wrong hands* before *you send it.* (On the other hand, that message you really *want* to retrieve will have been lost during a system crash.)

✦ Use the Bcc field sparingly. (A *Bcc* is a blind copy, a copy that's sent without the other recipients knowing about it.) For example, you may send e-mail to your boss with a Bcc to *his* boss. If she sends him a printed copy of your message, the fact that you sneaked behind his back is plainly visible in the header. Fortunately, your boss can't read headers, and you get away with it this time.

✦ Do use the Bcc field when you're sending mail to a long list of addresses. That way, each recipient doesn't have to wade through the entire list to read the message.

✦ Be careful when you're forwarding mail. Some mail addresses are really mailing lists that redistribute messages to many other people (including maybe your boss or your kids).

✦ Don't pass on chain letters like the one about the dying boy who wants greeting cards (he doesn't), the modem-tax rumor (a proposal squelched in 1987), the Good News or Good Times virus warning (a hoax), Bill Gates paying you for sending e-mail (not a chance), or any letter that offers you a way to make money fast just by putting your name at the bottom of the list and sending it to ten friends. (These moneymaking schemes are *always* illegal, are guaranteed to annoy your friends, and don't work.)

✦ Passing around jokes and lists of funny comments via e-mail has become quite popular. Make sure that friends want to receive those online humorgrams before you pass them on.

✦ Mass distribution of unsolicited e-mail, known as *spam,* is becoming more and more of a problem. Because most spammers use phony return addresses, replying with a complaint is usually a waste of time. In fact, your reply proves that your address is good, and may result in your receiving even more spam.

✦ Not every mail address has an actual person behind it. Some are mailing lists (***see also*** Part V), and some are *robots,* or *mailbots.* Mail robots have become popular as a way to query databases and retrieve files. (Messages to `idq6@gurus.com`, for example, are answered by our mailbot. Try it.)

✦ Unless you are using versions of Outlook Express and Windows 98 without the latest security updates, your computer cannot get a virus by reading a text e-mail message. However, you can infect your computer by opening files attached to e-mail. Don't *ever* open *any* file attached to messages from strangers or people you don't trust — or even from people you do know, if you're not expecting a file from them. Some viruses distribute themselves by sending messages to everyone in your e-mail program's address book, so the messages appear to be from a friend.

Finding e-mail addresses

Right now, no perfect way exists to find out someone's e-mail address. Here are the best options, though:

✦ Keep an e-mail address book. A word-processing file works fine if your mail program doesn't have this feature. When someone you care about sends you a message, copy her address, which is in the message's From field, and paste the address in your electronic address book.

✦ If you have the person's business card or stationery, see whether it lists an e-mail address.

✦ Call the person on the telephone and ask.

✦ AOL and other value-added services have ways for you to look up the addresses of other subscribers to that service. You have to be a subscriber on that provider's service, however. The address directory is one of the added values of a commercial service.

Several companies have set up Internet "white pages" directory services. You can register your e-mail address along with other information, such as your home page. They also allow you to search for telephone numbers. None is close to a complete list of e-mail addresses. Still, you can try any of these services to find long-lost friends or enemies:

✦ **Yahoo People Search:** `people.yahoo.com`

✦ **Switchboard:** `www.switchboard.com`

✦ **WhoWhere People Finder:** `www.whowhere.lycos.com`

Try using an Internet search engine, such as AltaVista (www.altavista.com) or Infoseek (www.infoseek.com). (*See also* Part VII.) Search for the name of the person or company whose e-mail address you want to find. Even people you wouldn't expect to be online are often listed somewhere on the Web.

Deja (www.deja.com) is particularly useful for finding someone who has posted a message in a Usenet newsgroup since 1995. If you don't find the person you're looking for, be sure to try a "power search" and search all the way back to the earliest days of the Deja database. (*See also* Part IV.)

Free e-mail

Some things in life *are* free. Several companies now offer free e-mail service. You just have to put up with onscreen advertising while you read your mail.

Most free e-mail services require that you have access to the Internet and have a Web browser. Web-based, free e-mail service is handy if you share a computer with other family members, want a way to access personal mail at work, or plan to switch e-mail providers. If you don't own a computer but have access to one at a public library, school, or cybercafé, you can still have a private e-mail address. Here are some Web-based free e-mail services:

✦ **MSN Hotmail:** www.hotmail.com

✦ **USA.NET Net@ddress:** www.netaddress.com

✦ **Switchboard Webmail:** webmail.switchboard.com

✦ **Yahoo! Mail:** mail.yahoo.com

HushMail (www.hushmail.com) offers free, Web-based e-mail with an important difference. HushMail users can send encrypted mail to each other, while receiving regular, unencrypted mail from other mail systems in the usual way. *See* "HushMail," in Part IX, for more information on encryption and how to use HushMail safely.

Juno (1-800-654-JUNO or www.juno.com) doesn't require that you have access to the Internet. You need a computer that can run Windows and a modem. Although you do have to pay for the phone calls, Juno has a network of access numbers throughout the United States. *See* "Using Juno," later in this part.

Headers

Headers are the lines of text that appear at the beginning of every Internet mail message. Use the following table as a guide to what these lines mean:

Subject	Describes message (recommended; sometimes required)
To	Lists recipients of the message (at least one required)
Cc	Lists carbon copy recipients (optional)
Bcc	Lists blind carbon copy recipients; these recipients' names are not sent with message (optional)
From	Address of message author (required; provided automatically)
Organization	Where the sender works, or whatever
X-Sender	Used with mailing lists to show who sent the message originally
Reply-To	Address to send replies to if it's different from the From line (optional)
Date	Time and date message was sent (provided automatically)
Expires	Date after which message expires (optional)
Message-ID	Unique, machine-generated identifier for message (provided automatically)
Lines	Number of text lines in message (optional; provided automatically)

Note: Many other optional header lines exist, although none of them is of great importance.

Rejected mail (bounces)

Every Internet host that can send or receive mail has a special mail address called `postmaster` that is supposed to be guaranteed to get a message to the person responsible for that host. If you send mail to someone and get back strange failure messages, you may try sending a polite message to the postmaster.

For example, if mail sent to `king@bluesuede.org` returns with an error, you may send e-mail to `postmaster@bluesuede.org` asking, "Does Elvis the King have a mailbox on this system? TIA, Ed Sullivan."

The postmaster is also the place to write if you believe that someone is seriously misusing a mail account. This action is the Internet equivalent of reporting someone to the police, so use it judiciously.

Because the postmaster is usually an overworked system administrator, it's considered poor form to pester her unnecessarily.

For more information about using e-mail, get a copy of *E-Mail For Dummies,* by John R. Levine, Carol Baroudi, Margaret Levine Young, and Arnold Reinhold (IDG Books Worldwide, Inc.). ***See also*** Chapters 11, 12, and 13 in *The Internet For Dummies,* 7th Edition, by John R. Levine, Carol Baroudi, and Margaret Levine Young (IDG Books Worldwide, Inc.).

Addresses

To send e-mail to someone, you need his address. Roughly speaking, mail addresses consist of these elements:

✦ **Mailbox name:** Usually, the username of your account.

✦ **@:** The *at* sign.

✦ **Host name:** The name of his computer. ***See also*** "Host names and domain names," later in this section.

For example, elvis@gurus.com is a typical address, where elvis is the mailbox name and gurus.com is the host name.

Internet mailbox names should *not* contain commas, spaces, or parentheses.

Mailbox names can contain letters, numerals, and, some punctuation characters, such as periods, hyphens, and underscores. Capitalization normally doesn't matter in e-mail addresses.

The most common situation in which these restrictions cause problems is in numeric CompuServe addresses, which consist of two numbers separated by a comma. When you're converting a CompuServe address to an Internet address, change the comma to a period. For example, the address 71053,2615 becomes 71053.2615@compuserve.com as an e-mail address. Similarly, some AOL users put spaces in their screen names. You just drop the spaces when you're sending the e-mail. If, for some reason, you must send mail to an address that does include commas, spaces, or parentheses, enclose the address in double quotes.

"What's my address?"

If you're accessing the Internet through a service provider, your address is most likely

your_login_name@your_provider's_host_name

If you're connected through work or school, your e-mail address is typically

your_login_name@your_computer's_host_name

A host name, however, is sometimes just a department or company name rather than your computer's name. If your login name is elvis and your computer is shamu.strat.gurus.org, your mail address may look like one of these examples:

```
elvis@shamu.strat.gurus.com
elvis@strat.gurus.com
elvis@gurus.com
```

or even this one:

```
elvis.presley@gurus.com
```

If you're using a computer that isn't connected to the Internet all the time, your mail is probably handled by a central mail server. As a result, you should use your login name — the name you use when you contact the mail server.

If you're not sure what your mail address is, send a message to Internet For Dummies Central, at idq6@gurus.com, and our robot will send back a note containing the address from which your message was sent, which is your mail address. While you're at it, add a sentence or two telling us how you like this book. (We read all our mail, although not always in the same month you send it.)

To find out someone else's e-mail address, *see also* "Finding e-mail addresses," earlier in this part.

Host names and domain names

Hosts are computers that are directly attached to the Internet.

Host names have several parts strung together with periods, like this:

```
ivan.iecc.com
```

You decode a host name from right to left:

✦ The rightmost part of a name is its *top-level domain,* or *TLD* (in the preceding example, com). *See also* "Top-level domains," later in this part.

✦ To the TLD's left (iecc) is the name of the company, school, or organization.

✦ The part to the left of the organization name (ivan) identifies the particular computer within the organization.

In large organizations, host names can be further subdivided by site or department.

The last two hunks of a host name are known as a *domain.* For example, ivan is in the iecc.com domain, and iecc.com is a *domain name.*

Most domain names in the United States are assigned by Network Solutions (www.networksolutions.com) and cost $70 to register and $35 per year after the first two years. Other registrars, like

Internet Domain Registrars (www.registrars.com) and Joker (www.joker.com) are cheaper and do at least as good a job. For a list of organizations that can register a domain name for you, see this URL:

www.icann.org/registrars/accredited-list.html

Internet Service Providers often charge substantial additional fees for setting up and supporting a new domain. Shop around!

IP addresses and DNS

Network software uses the IP address, which is sort of like a phone number, to identify the host. IP addresses are written in four chunks separated by periods, such as

208.31.42.77

A system called the *domain name system* (*DNS*) keeps track of which IP address (or addresses, for popular Internet hosts) goes with which Internet host name. Usually, one computer has one IP address and one Internet host name, although this isn't always true. For example, the Web site at www.yahoo.com is so heavily used that a group of computers, each with its own IP address, accept requests for Web pages from that name.

The most important IP addresses to know are the IP addresses of the computers at the Internet provider you use. You may need them in order to set up the software on your computer; if things get fouled up, the IP addresses will help the guru who fixes your problem.

Top-level domains

The *top-level domain (TLD),* sometimes called a *zone*, is the last piece of the host name on the Internet (for example, the zone of gurus.com is com). TLDs come in two main flavors:

✦ Organizational

✦ Geographical

If the TLD is three or more letters long, it's an *organizational name.* The following table describes the organizational names that have been in use for years:

com	Commercial organization
edu	Educational institution, usually a college or university
gov	U.S. government body or department
int	International organization (mostly NATO, at the moment)

mil	U.S. military site (can be located anywhere)
net	Networking organization
org	Anything that doesn't fit elsewhere, usually a not-for-profit group

It used to be that most systems using organizational names were in the United States. The com domain has now become a hot property; large corporations and organizations worldwide consider it a prestige Internet address. Address haves and have-nots are contesting a plan to add additional top-level domain names to those already in use.

If the TLD is two letters long, it's a *geographical name.* The 2-letter code specifies a country, like uk for the United Kingdom, au for Australia, and jp for Japan. **See also** the appendix for a full list.

The stuff in front of the TLD is specific to that country. Often, the letter group just before the country code mimics the style for U.S. organizational names: com or co for commercial, edu or ac for academic institutions, and gov or go for government, for example.

Some countries are selling domain names in their TLDs to all comers. These vanity TLDs include cc, to, tu, tv, and uz.

The us domain — used by schools, cities, and small organizations in the United States — is set up strictly geographically. The two letters just before us specify the state. Other common codes are ci for city, co for county, cc for community colleges, and k12 for schools.

The Internet site for the city of Cambridge, Massachusetts, for example, is www.ci.cambridge.ma.us.

A host can have more than one name. John's machine in Trumansburg, New York, is known as ivan.iecc.com, iecc. trumansburg.ny.us, net.gurus.com, and www.greattapes. com.

Port numbers

Internet host computers can run many programs at one time, and they can have simultaneous network connections to lots of other computers. The different connections are kept straight by *port numbers,* which identify particular programs on a computer. For example:

✦ File transfer (FTP) uses port 21.

✦ E-mail uses port 25.

✦ The Web uses port 80.

Your file transfer, e-mail, or newsgroup program should automatically select the correct port to use, so you don't need to know these port numbers. Now and then, you see a port number as part of an Internet address (URL). For example, the U.S. National Security Agency home page is

`www.nsa.gov:8080/`

where 8080 is the port number. You don't have to do anything special; just copy the URL as written.

URLs versus e-mail addresses

URLs (Uniform Resource Locators) contain the information your browser software uses to find Web pages on the World Wide Web. URLs look somewhat like e-mail addresses in that both contain a domain name. E-mail addresses almost always contain an @, however, and URLs never do. *See also* "Uniform Resource Locators (URLs)," in Part VI.

E-mail addresses are usually not case sensitive — capitalization doesn't matter — but parts of URLs *are* case-sensitive. Always type URLs *exactly* as written, including capitalization.

URLs that appear in newspapers and magazines sometimes have an extra hyphen added at the end of a line when the URL continues on the next line. If the URL doesn't work as written, try deleting that hyphen.

America Online and CompuServe Addresses

America Online and CompuServe have their own mail-addressing schemes. Here's how to address Internet messages to these systems:

✦ For America Online (AOL) users, the address is `username@aol.com`. If the member's name has a space in it, just delete the space. For example, "Jane Doe" becomes `JaneDoe@aol.com`.

✦ For CompuServe, users have a numeric address and a username. A numeric address is in the format *nnnnn,nnnn* (two numbers separated by a comma); turn this into an Internet e-mail address by changing the comma to a period and adding `@compuserve.com` to the end (`userid.userid@compuserve.com`). For example, if the person's CompuServe ID is 76543,210, send mail to `76543.210@compuserve.com`. If you know someone's username, just add `@compuserve.com` to the end.

Attachments

To send a file by e-mail, you *attach* it to an e-mail message. Compose and address the message as usual by using your e-mail program, and then use the program's toolbar or commands to attach the file to the message. You can attach more than one file to a message, but don't send files that are too large — your recipient's mail system may choke on large files. To send a file larger than 100K, use a compression program (like WinZip or ZipMagic) to make the file smaller.

 Before you send someone an attached file, make sure that he wants it. Ask for permission to send the file, and ask whether the recipient has the necessary program to open the file you're sending. For example, if you're sending a Microsoft Word document, the recipient of the file needs a program that can open a Word document.

 E-mail programs use one of three methods of encoding an attached file so that it can travel through the e-mail system: MIME, uuencoding, and BinHex. MIME is the most widely used encoding system.

 Web sites that offer free disk storage space you can share with friends are a useful alternative to e-mail attachments for large files. *See also* "Free, free, free," in Part VII.

Smileys and Emoticons

Smileys and emoticons substitute for the inflection of voice that is missing in e-mail messages. *Smileys* are supposed to look like faces when you turn your head sideways. *Emoticons* are not pictorial; they're hints about the writer's feelings or actions. Because smileys and emoticons are still the e-mail equivalent of slang, you probably shouldn't use them in a formal message at work. Here are some common ones:

:-) or :)	The basic smiley
;-)	Winking; "Don't hit me for what I just said!"
:-(	Frowning
:->	Sarcastic
8-)	Wearing sunglasses
::-)	Wears glasses normally
;-(	Crying
:-@	Screaming
:-o	Uh-oh!

(continued)

<g> or <grin>	Same as :-)
<sigh>	Sigh!
88	Love and kisses (from ham radio)
\,,/	I love you (from American Sign Language)
::	Action markers, as in ::picks up hammer and smashes monitor::

Lots and lots more smileys are used, with many Web pages devoted to them. Check our Web site, at net.gurus.com/smileys.html, for some suggested current lists.

Using America Online (AOL)

When you send mail from your AOL account, you can address it to either another AOL user (by typing the user's screen name) or an Internet address (by typing the Internet address). Internet users can send you e-mail by leaving the spaces out of your screen name (account name) and adding @aol.com to the end. If your AOL account name is Steve Case, for example, your Internet address is SteveCase@aol.com. This information applies to AOL 5.0 for Windows, although the Macintosh version is very similar.

Finding an address

To find the address of an AOL member, choose People⇨Search AOL Member Directory from the toolbar (or type **member directory** in the white box below the toolbar). In the Member Directory window, type what you know about the person and click the Search button.

Reading incoming mail

1. Click the Read button on the toolbar (the leftmost icon) or the You Have Mail icon in the Welcome window. Your Online Mailbox window appears.

2. Highlight the message on the list.

3. Click Read or press Enter. AOL displays the message.

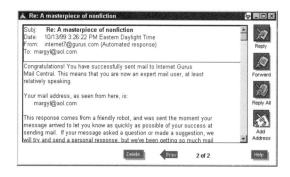

4. To place the address of the sender in your AOL address book, click Add Address.

5. Click the Next button to see the next message.

To help combat spam (junk e-mail), AOL suggests that you forward unsolicited, commercial e-mail to TOSSpam. AOL also has a nifty feature that lets you limit the amount of junk mail you receive by restricting incoming mail to AOL users and Internet sites you select. Type the keyword **mail controls**. Just make sure that you don't block mail from people you *do* want to hear from.

AOL has a handy feature called Automatic AOL that lets you read your e-mail messages offline (this feature used to be called Flash Sessions). If you pay a flat monthly rate for AOL, this feature is less important. It comes in handy, however, if you're paying for telephone connect-time, don't want to tie up the phone, or aren't using the AOL flat-rate plan. Choose Mail Center⇨Set Up Automatic AOL from the toolbar to tell AOL when you retrieve your mail. Then choose Mail Center⇨Run Automatic AOL to get your mail.

Sending new mail

1. Click the Write icon on the toolbar.

The Write Mail window appears.

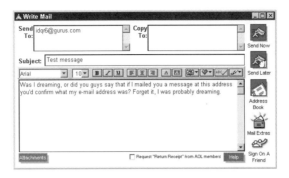

2. Type the recipient's address in the Send To box.

3. Type in the Copy To box the addresses of anyone else you want to send this message to.

4. Fill in the Subject box.

5. Type your message in the main box. To find those pesky typos, click the Spell Check button (with the letters ABC on it).

If you're sending a message to another AOL user, you can use the buttons along the top of the main box to add boldface, italics, and other fancy formatting to your message. If you're sending a message to Internet users, don't bother with formatting unless you know that their mailer is compatible. Most aren't.

6. If you want to send a file along with the message, click the Attachments button and choose the file to attach.

7. After you're done, click Send Now or Send Later. Clicking Send Later holds your mail in an outbox for later transmission.

You can press the Tab key to go from box to box in AOL windows.

AOL sends file attachments in MIME format. The contents of the attached file don't usually appear as part of the message. Instead, the file shows up as a separate file on the recipient's hard disk.

If you change your mind about attaching the document, click the Attachments button, select the file you don't want to send, and click Detach.

You can add a *signature* to the end of the message automatically, so you don't have to type your standard closing each time you send a message. Click the Signature button (at the right end of the row of icons in the Write Mail window) and choose Set up Signatures from the menu that appears. You can create several different signatures — for example, one for business-related messages and another for messages that relate to the fantasy baseball league you run.

Replying to messages

1. While reading a message, click the Reply icon in the message window.

A mail window appears with the Send To box and the Subject box filled in. You can edit the subject, if you like.

2. Type your message in the main box.

3. After you're done, click the Send Now or Send Later button.

Forwarding messages

1. While reading a message, click the Forward icon in the message window.

A mail window appears with the Subject filled in. You can edit the subject, if you want. The original message doesn't appear in this window, although it's included in the message you send.

2. Type the recipient's address in the Send To box.

3. Type in the Copy To box the addresses of anyone else you want to send this message to.

4. Add a comment, if you like, in the main box.

5. After you're done, click the Send Now or Send Later icon.

Saving messages

1. Display the message you want onscreen.

2. Choose File⇨Save As.

3. Enter the filename you want to save this message in.

4. Click Save to save your message as a text file.

You can also save messages to your AOL Personal Filing Cabinet, which is stored on your computer. Choose File⇨Save to Personal Filing Cabinet from the menu.

Using Eudora (Windows and Mac)

Eudora is a popular e-mail program you can use with any SLIP or PPP Internet account. It runs on Windows 3.1, Windows 95, Windows 98, and the Mac. Two versions of Eudora are available from www.eudora.com: a freeware version named Eudora Light and a more complete commercial (but inexpensive) version named Eudora Pro. Eudora Pro includes a spell checker and can download

mail in the background while you're reading and composing messages. Except where noted, we describe Eudora Light 3.0 for
Windows and 3.1 for the Mac.

If you live in the United States or Canada and you want to protect
your e-mail from prying eyes, download the PGP encryption plug-in
from www.pgp.com (*see* Part IX).

Configuring Eudora

After you install Eudora (Light or Pro), you have to tell the program
how to pick up and send your mail. Ask your Internet Service
Provider for the names of your SMTP server (for outgoing mail).
Then configure Eudora:

1. Choose Tools⇨Options from the menu bar.

You see the Options dialog box, with a column of category
icons or names down the left side.

2. Click the Personal Information icon and fill in the POP account
(your e-mail address), Real name, and Return address (type
your e-mail address again) boxes. Leave the Dialup username
box blank. In Eudora Pro, click the Getting Started icon and fill
in the Return address and Real name.

3. Click the Hosts icon (the Sending Mail icon in Eudora Pro) and
fill in the SMTP server box with the host name of your Internet
service provider's (ISP's) mail server. (Call your ISP if you don't
know.)

4. Click OK to save your configuration settings.

Getting incoming mail

1. Choose File⇨Check Mail or press Ctrl+M. (In Eudora Pro, you
can also click the Check Mail icon on the toolbar.)

Eudora dials up your account (if you're not already connected)
and downloads to your PC any mail you have.

2. If you have mail, Eudora displays a message and alerts you with
a sound. Click OK to make the message go away.

Eudora can create filters that automatically check incoming messages against a list of senders and subjects and file them in appropriate mailboxes. Choose Special⇨Filters in Eudora Lite or Tools⇨
Filters in Eudora Pro.

Reading incoming mail

1. When Eudora starts, it displays its In folder, showing a list of all
your mail, if you have any. If it doesn't display this list, choose

Mailbox⇨In or press Ctrl+I. (In Eudora Light, you can also click the In icon on the toolbar; in Eudora Pro, click the Open In Mailbox icon.)

2. To read a message, double-click its line on the list.

The message appears in a window.

To add this person's address in your Eudora address book, choose S Address Book Entry.

3. When you're done reading the message, close its window.

Sending new mail

1. Choose Message⇨New Message, press Ctrl+M, or click the New Message button on the toolbar.

Eudora pops up a new message window.

2. Type the recipient's e-mail address on the To line.

3. Press Tab to skip to the Subject line.

4. Press Tab a few more times to skip the Cc and Bcc lines (or type the addresses of people who should get courtesy copies and blind copies of the message).

5. In the large text area, type your message.

Send

6. To send the message, click the button in the upper-right corner of the message window — which, depending on how Eudora is configured, is marked Send or Queue.

If you click Send, Eudora sends the message immediately. If you click Queue, your message is stashed in your Outbox folder for transmission later, when you connect to your Internet provider.

Replying to messages

Reply

1. After reading a message, choose Message⇨Reply, press Ctrl+R, or click the Reply icon on the toolbar.

Eudora pops up a message window with the recipient's address filled in and the recipient's message displayed. Each line of the original message appears in the message box, preceded by a > character.

2. Type your reply. Be sure to edit the original message so that only the important parts remain.

3. To send the message, click the button in the upper-right corner of the window labeled Send or Queue.

Forwarding messages

1. After reading a message, choose <u>M</u>essage➪<u>F</u>orward or click the Forward icon on the toolbar.

Eudora pops up a message window with the current message displayed. Each line is preceded with a > character.

If you don't want the > characters, choose Message➪Redirect instead.

2. Type the recipient's e-mail address.

3. Edit the original message or add more text, if you want.

4. To send the message, click the Send or Queue button in the upper-right corner of the window, just like you do when you're sending a new message.

Saving messages

1. Select the message by bringing its window to the front or by clicking its line in the In window.

2. Choose T<u>r</u>ansfer from the menu bar and then choose a mailbox from the Transfer menu.

You can create additional mailboxes by choosing Transfer➪New.

Reading saved messages

1. Choose Mailbo<u>x</u> from the menu bar and then select the mailbox from the Mailbo<u>x</u> menu.

2. Double-click the message in the mailbox window that appears.

Attaching a file

1. Compose the message as usual.

You can compose a new message by clicking the New Message icon on the toolbar, or you can reply to or forward a message. You can attach a file to any message you send with Eudora.

2. Choose <u>M</u>essage➪Attac<u>h</u> File from the menu bar or press Ctrl+H. (In Eudora Pro, you can also click the Attach File button on the toolbar.)

3. In the Attach File dialog box, choose the directory and filename of the file to attach and click OK.

On the toolbar for the message, the third box from the left shows which kind of encoding Eudora plans to use. The box usually shows a clown face, indicating that the file will be sent as a MIME attachment.

4. To change the encoding, click the arrow button to its right and choose a different type (MIME or BinHex). Use MIME unless you know that your recipient can handle only BinHex. (In Eudora Pro, you can also send messages by using uuencoding.) *See also* Part VII.

5. Send the message as usual.

The contents of the attached file don't appear as part of the message. The file is "stapled" to the message but remains separate.

If you change your mind about attaching the document, click the filename in the message header and press the Delete key to delete it.

You may think that, rather than choose Message⊸Attach File, you can just type directly in the header of your message the directory and filename of the file you want to attach. But, no! Eudora doesn't let you do that, and we don't know why.

Incoming attachments are automatically saved to files, and the name and location of each saved file are shown at the end of the message. On Macs and on PCs using Windows 95 and Windows NT, Eudora Pro also shows the file as an icon you can double-click to open.

Using Juno (Windows)

Juno is a service that lets you send and receive e-mail from the Internet — *for free!* You just have to put up with the ads Juno displays while you're reading your mail, and you have to be in the U.S. Unlike other free e-mail services, Juno does not require that you have Internet access. You need a computer that can run Windows — Windows 3.1, Windows 95, or Windows 98 — as well as a 9600 bps or faster modem. Juno has more than 2,300 access numbers throughout the United States. You have to pay for any telephone charges. (If you use Windows 3.1, you must install the older Version 1.49 instead).

Getting and installing Juno Software

To use Juno, you have to install special Juno software on your PC — this book describes Juno Version 3.0 with the free Juno basic service. You can download the Juno software from www.juno.com or get a copy from a friend who has Juno — it encourages this method. Juno mails you a disk if you call, at 800-654-JUNO (in the United States). This disk isn't free, however. If you use Windows 3.1, download an older version (version 1.49) instead. Juno has no versions for DOS or Macs.

To install Juno:

1. Follow the directions that come with Juno or double-click the file junoinst.exe.

2. Make sure that your modem is turned on and not in use or that your LAN or cable connection to the Internet is working.

3. Click the Create New Account button to set up your user pro-file. You can choose between Juno basic service (e-mail only, for free), Juno Gold (e-mail only, but allows attachments, for about $3 per month), or Juno Web (using Juno as your ISP, for about $20 per month).

Juno asks you to answer roughly 20 questions about your tastes, interests, and demographics to help it select which advertisements to show you. Juno says: "While we make available to our advertis-ers a great deal of statistical information about our member base, we never share information about any individual member without that member's permission." Permission can be implied by your responses to ads, however.

Reading incoming mail

1. To see whether you have new mail, make sure that your modem is turned on and not in use.

2. Start Juno and click Yes in the Check for New mail dialog box. If Juno is already running, click the Get New Mail button on the Read tab. If you have outgoing mail waiting to be sent, Juno asks whether you want to send it while you're online. When Juno is finished getting your mail, it displays a count of what it received (and sent).

3. Click Close. If you have e-mail waiting for you, you see a count of how many unread messages are in the folder information window. A scrolling list of messages appears below that, show-ing the sender, subject, date, and status of each message.

4. Click a listed message to see its text in the lower-right part of the Juno window.

Composing and sending new mail

Normally, you compose messages on your computer and then dial in to Juno to send them:

1. Start Juno and click the Write tab. You see a new, blank message.

2. Type the recipient's Internet address or alias in the Send to box.

3. If you want, type additional recipients' Internet addresses or aliases in the Cc box.

4. Fill in the Subject box.

5. Type your message in the large text box.

You can't send file attachments using the free service; you have to sign up for Juno Gold.

6. Check the spelling in your message by clicking the Spell Check button.

7. Click the Send Mail button. You can either save the message in your Outbox for later transmission by clicking Put Mail in Outbox or click Get and Send Mail Now for immediate gratification.

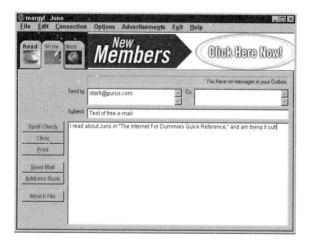

If you want to keep a copy of all the messages you send, choose Options⇨E-mail Options from the Juno menu to display the E-mail Options dialog box; make sure that the Save All Send Mail setting is selected. Otherwise, Juno discards outgoing mail after sending it.

If you decide not to send a message that you've composed, click the Clear button rather than the Send Mail button.

Replying to messages

1. When you're reading a message, click the Reply button. You see the Reply Settings dialog box.

2. Choose whether you want your reply to go to only the sender or to all recipients. Select whether Juno should include in your reply the text of the original message.

Juno displays a new message window, with the address and subject lines already filled in. If you asked to include the original message, it appears preceded by > characters.

3. Type your reply. Check your spelling by clicking the Spell Chec_k_ button.

4. Click the _S_end Mail button.

Forwarding messages

1. When you're reading a message, click the Forward button.

Juno displays a new message window, with the subject already filled in. The original message appears at the bottom of the window.

2. Type the address of the recipient in the To box.

3. Type any additional text you want to include.

4. Click the _S_end Mail button.

Using the address book

Juno gives you a personal address book that can automatically store the addresses of everyone who sends you e-mail. To open the address book, click the _A_ddress Book button on the Read or Write tab.

In the Address Book window, click the New _N_ame button to add an entry. Juno asks for the person's first name, last name, e-mail address, and an *alias.* You use the alias in the To or Cc field as a nickname in place of the person's e-mail address. When you're done looking at the address book, click OK.

When you're composing a message or addressing a message you're forwarding, click the _A_ddress Book button, select a name, and click the _S_end To or Cop_y_ To buttons. Juno automatically enters the person's address in the appropriate field of your message. Click OK to return to your message.

You can sort the address book by name, e-mail address, or alias by clicking the gray bar at the top of the appropriate column. To create a list of people to whom you send messages, enter each person into the address book, click New _L_ist, and choose the people to include on the list.

Saving messages in a folder

1. When you're reading a message, click the Mo<u>v</u>e to Folder button.

You see the Move to Folder dialog box.

2. Select an existing folder or create a new one by typing its name in the Move Message Into box.

3. Click OK.

The Copy to Folder button lets you save a message in more than one folder. To read the messages in a folder, choose its name from the Folder drop-down list.

Using Netscape Messenger (Windows, Mac, Linux, and UNIX)

Netscape Communicator (version 4.0 and later) includes an e-mail program named Netscape Messenger. You can use Netscape with any PPP account, and versions are available for Windows 3.1, Windows 98 and Windows 95, Macs, Linux, and UNIX. This book describes version 4.7. (If you have an earlier version of Netscape, download a newer one from home.netscape.com.)

Setting up Netscape for e-mail

Ask your ISP for the names of your SMTP server (for outgoing mail) and your POP server (for incoming mail). Follow these steps to configure Netscape:

1. Choose <u>C</u>ommunicator⇨<u>M</u>essenger from the Netscape menu bar.

Ignore any nasty message about being unable to use the POP server. You're about to tell it how. If Netscape asks whether you want to make it your default e-mail application, click Yes if you plan to use Messenger as your regular e-mail program, and No if you're just trying it out. You see the Netscape Messenger window (which says something like *Netscape Communications Services* on the title bar).

2. Choose <u>E</u>dit⇨Mail Server Pr<u>o</u>perties to display the Preferences dialog box with the Mail & Newsgroups tab selected.

Other types of settings are listed down the left side of the window.

3. Click the Mail Servers category.

You see settings for your incoming and outgoing mail. You can tell Messenger to collect incoming mail from one or more POP servers and to send your outgoing mail to one SMTP server.

4. If a server named *xxx* appears on the Incoming Mail Servers list, click Edit to configure it. If not, tell Messenger to get your mail from your POP server by clicking the Add button.

Either way, you see the Mail Server Properties dialog box, with information about your POP server.

5. In the Server Name box, type the name of your ISP's POP server. In the User Name box, type your username (the part of your e-mail address before the @).

If you want Messenger to remember your password after you've typed it once, click the Remember Password box. If you want the program to check your mail at regular intervals, click the Check For Mail Every box, and type a number.

6. Click OK. You return to the Preferences dialog box.

7. In the Outgoing Mail (SMTP) Server box, type the name of your ISP's SMTP mail server.

8. Click the Identity category on the list along the left side of the Preferences dialog box.

You see another screen full of options.

9. Fill in the Your Name box with what you want to appear in the From field of all your messages; for example:

`Arnold G. Reinhold`

10. Enter your full e-mail address in the Email Address field.

11. If you want to have a signature added automatically to all your messages, create a text file with the signature in it (containing as many as three lines of text, including your name and e-mail address). Type its name in the Signature File box in this window or click the Choose button to locate the file. If you don't want to add a signature to your messages, leave the Signature File box blank.

12. Click OK to dismiss the Preferences dialog box.

13. To test your settings, try getting your incoming mail (as described in the following section).

Getting and reading incoming mail

1. If you don't already see Messenger's Mail window, choose Communicator⇨Messenger from the menu bar.

2. Click the Get Messages button or press Ctrl+T.

Get Msg

If Netscape gets your mail automatically when you open the Netscape Messenger window, skip this step. Messenger lists your folders along the left side of the window, under the heading Local Mail. Click Local Mail if the list of folders doesn't appear.

3. Click the Inbox folder to see your incoming messages in the upper-right part of the Messenger window.

You can adjust the width of the left column (the list of mail folders) windows by dragging the ends of the column labels.

4. Click a message to read it.

The new message appears in the lower-right part of the window. If you double-click the message on the list of messages, the message text appears in a new window. You can also use the Next and Previous buttons to skim through your messages.

Sending new mail

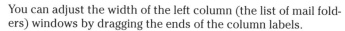

1. Press Ctrl+M or click the New Message button on the toolbar.

Netscape pops up a Composition window.

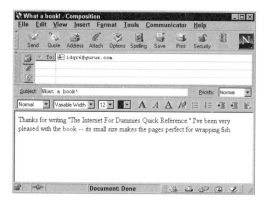

2. Type the recipient's e-mail address in the To box. You can enter more than one address if you put a comma after each one.

3. If you want, click the blank box below the To button to make a box for Cc or Bcc addresses. You can also click the address book icon to choose an address from your personal address book.

4. Enter a few informative words in the Subject box.

5. In the large area, type your message.

Attach

6. If you want to attach a file to the message, click the Attach button on the toolbar and choose File from the menu that appears (or choose File⇨Attach⇨File from the menu bar). Choose the file to attach and click the Open button.

The filename appears on the list of attached files on the Attachment tab.

Send

7. Click the Send button or press Ctrl+Enter to send the message. If you want to send the message later, choose File⇨Send Later.

Netscape sends attached files by using the MIME format.

Replying to messages

Reply

1. Display the message you want to reply to and then press Ctrl+R or click the Reply icon on the toolbar. If you want the reply to be addressed to everyone who received the original message, click the Reply All icon.

Netscape pops up a Composition window with the recipient's address filled in. The recipient's message is displayed with each line of the original message preceded by > or | characters. (If the message doesn't appear, click the Quote icon.)

2. Delete the boring parts of the original message so that only the important parts remain.

3. Type your reply.

4. Click the Send button to send the message.

Forwarding messages

Forward

1. After reading a message, choose Message⇨Forward, press Ctrl+L, or click the Forward icon on the toolbar.

Netscape pops up a Composition window with the current message displayed. (If it's not, click the Quote icon on the toolbar.)

2. Type the recipient's e-mail address.

3. Edit the original message or add more text, if you want.

4. Click the Send button to send the message.

Saving messages in folders

Netscape Messenger comes with some folders — Inbox, Unsent Messages, Drafts, Templates, Sent, and Trash — and you can also make your own. To create a new folder, right-click the Local Mail entry in the list of folders and choose <u>N</u>ew Folder from the menu that appears (or choose <u>F</u>ile⇔New <u>F</u>older from the menu bar). When you type a name for the folder, it appears with your other folders.

To move a message from one folder to another (for example, from the Inbox folder to your Love Letters folder), drag the message from the list of messages to the folder where you want it saved. Or select the message and choose <u>M</u>essage⇔<u>M</u>ove from the menu bar, and choose the folder to which you want to move the message.

Reading saved messages

1. Click the name of the folder that contains the message you want to read. The messages in that folder appear in the upper-right part of the Messenger window.

2. Click the message.

Using Outlook Express (Windows and Mac)

Windows 98 and Internet Explorer 5.0 come with a built-in mail program named Outlook Express 5.0. A version of Outlook Express is also available for the Macintosh. You can set up Outlook Express to work with many different mail services. To run Outlook Express, click to open its icon on your Windows desktop or taskbar. If the program asks whether you want to dial a connection, choose not to dial a connection if you want to work offline or choose the Internet account with which you want to send and receive mail.

In the Outlook Express window, the list of folders (including your Inbox, Outbox, and others) appears down the left side of the window. The upper-right part of the window displays the list of messages in the selected folder, and the lower part shows the selected message.

Outlook Express is not the same as Outlook 97, Outlook 98, or Outlook 2000, which come with Microsoft Office.

Getting and reading incoming mail

1. To get your mail, click the Send and Receive button on the toolbar.

Send and Receive

If you're not already connected to your Internet account, Outlook Express connects you (it may display the Dial-Up Connecting or other window to get your password). Then it sends any messages you've composed and gets your new messages.

2. To see the messages in your inbox, click Inbox on the list of folders on the left side of the Outlook Express window or choose Go⇨Inbox from the menu bar.

A list of messages appears in the upper-right part of the Outlook Express window. Messages you haven't read yet appear in bold.

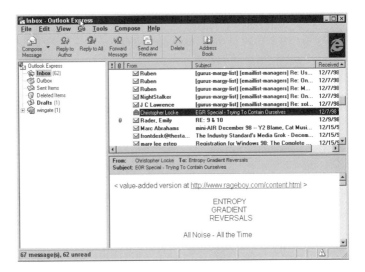

3. To read a message, click it. The text of the message appears in the lower-right part of the Outlook Express window. To display the message in its own window, double-click it.

 Messages may include icons in the text. Click an icon to see the picture, view the Web page, or run the program the icon represents.

 Don't click icons for programs from people or organizations you don't know! Even if you do know the sender, don't open documents or run programs that you didn't expect the person to send: A virus on your friend's computer may have sent you a virus-laden file.

Sending new mail

1. To create a new message, click the Compose Message button on the toolbar or choose Compose⇨New Message or press Ctrl+N.

You see the New Message window.

2. On the To line, type the address to which to send the message. To select recipients from your address book, click the Rolodex-style index card icon to the left of the box.

If you want to send copies to anyone, type the e-mail address on the Cc line. To send copies without other recipients knowing it, type addresses on the Bcc line.

3. Type the subject of the message on the Subject line.

4. In the box in the lower half of the New Message window, type the text of your message. If you're sending the message to someone who you're *sure* can receive formatted e-mail, use the formatting buttons right above the message area to format your text; otherwise, leave those buttons alone!

5. Check the spelling of your message by pressing F7 or choosing Tools⇨Spelling from the menu bar.

6. If you want to attach a file to the message, click the Insert File button (the one with a little paper clip) on the toolbar. In the Insert Attachment window that appears, choose the file to attach and click Attach.

7. Click the Send button to send the message.

To cancel sending a message (before you've clicked the Send button), just close the window.

Replying to messages

1. To reply to a message and send your reply to everyone who received the original message, click the Reply to All button on the toolbar. (If you want to send your reply to only the person who sent the message, click the Reply to Author button instead.)

You see a message composition window in which the To line already shows the addresses you want to send the reply to, and the Subject line is already filled in too. The text of the original message appears in the message area.

2. Delete all the parts of the original message that are boring — the parts that don't pertain to your reply. Then type your reply.

3. Send the message by clicking the Send button on the toolbar.

Forwarding messages

Forward
Message

1. To forward a message you've received, click the Forward Message button on the toolbar.

You see a message composition window, with the text of the original message in the message area and the subject already filled in.

2. Type the address (or addresses) to which you want to send the message. (To select them from your address book, click the little Rolodex-style index card icon to the left of the To box.)

3. Type an additional message in the message area, if you want.

4. Send the message by clicking the Send button.

Saving messages in folders

You can create folders by highlighting Outlook Express on the list of folders and then choosing File⇨Folder⇨New Folder from the menu and typing the folder's name. To move a message from your Inbox to another folder, drag it from the list of messages to the other folder (as listed on the left side of the Outlook Express window).

To save in a file the message you're looking at, choose File⇨Save As from the menu.

To see the messages in a folder, click that folder on the list of folder names.

Using Pine (Linux and UNIX)

Pine is (in our humble opinion) the best mail reader for UNIX systems. Like most UNIX programs, Pine uses commands that are single keystrokes — no mouse, no muss, no fuss.

Running Pine

1. To run Pine, type **pine**. You see the Pine main menu. Type **?** for help.

2. When you're done with Pine, press **q** to quit.

Pine asks whether you really, really want to quit.

3. Press **y** to leave.

If you left messages in your inbox that you have read but not deleted, Pine asks whether you want to move the messages to your read-messages folder — press **y** or **n**. If you deleted messages, Pine asks whether you really want to delete them. Again, press **y** or **n**.

Reading incoming mail

1. Press **i** to see the messages in the current folder, which is usually the Incoming folder.

2. To read a message, move the highlight to it and press **v** or Enter.

3. To delete the current message, press **d**. To go to the next message without deleting this one, press **n**.

4. After you're done, press **m** to return to the main menu.

Sending new mail

1. Press **c** to compose a message.

You see a blank message.

2. Enter the addresses and the subject line.

3. If you want to attach a file to a message, enter the filename on the Attchmnt: (attachment) line.

4. Type the text of the message.

5. When you're ready to send the message, press Ctrl+X.

Pine asks whether you really want to send the message.

6. Press **y**.

7. Press **s** to send the message. Press **f** if you don't want to send it.

Pine sends the message and displays the main menu again.

Replying to messages

1. Display the message onscreen.

2. Press **r**.

You see the same screen you see when you're composing a new message, with the address and subject filled in.

3. Edit the message and send the reply the same way as you send a new message. ***See also*** the preceding section, "Sending new mail."

Forwarding messages

1. Display the message onscreen.

2. Press **f** to forward the message.

You see the same screen you see when you're composing a new message, with the subject and text of the message filled in.

3. Edit and send the message the same way you send a new message. ***See also*** "Sending new mail," earlier in this section.

Saving messages to a file

1. Display the message onscreen.

2. Press **e**.

Pine asks for the filename in which to save the message (it puts the file in your home directory).

3. Enter the filename and press Enter.

Usenet Newsgroups

Usenet, also known as *network news,* is a worldwide distributed group-discussion system. Internet users around the world submit Usenet messages to tens of thousands of *newsgroups* with names like `rec.gardens.orchids` and `sci.space`. Within a day or so, these messages are delivered to nearly every other Internet host that wants them for anyone to read.

In this part . . .

- ✔ Deja.com and Usenet indexers
- ✔ Frequently Asked Questions (FAQs)
- ✔ Newsgroup names
- ✔ Newsgroup netiquette
- ✔ Posting your first article
- ✔ Ramping up your own newsgroup
- ✔ Reading newsgroups with America Online
- ✔ Reading newsgroups with Deja.com
- ✔ Reading newsgroups with Netscape Newsgroup
- ✔ Reading newsgroups with Outlook Express
- ✔ Reading newsgroups with other newsreaders

Reading Usenet — a huge system of Internet-based bulletin boards — is like trying to drink from a fire hose. Usenet had more than 25,000 different newsgroups last we looked. Here are some tips for maintaining your sanity:

✦ Pick a few groups that really interest you or use an indexing service like Deja.com.

✦ Avoid the hot political groups unless you have an ample supply of Valium.

✦ Develop a tolerance for the numerous junk-mail messages that infest many groups.

✦ If you feel that you absolutely have to reply to a comment, save the message and sleep on it. If it still seems urgent in the morning, see "Posting Your First Article," later in this part.

✦ Don't get into a flame war; if ever you do, however, let the other guy have the last word.

✦ Don't believe everything you read on Usenet.

To read newsgroups postings, you use a *newsreader* program, or you can use your browser to read newsgroup postings on the Deja.com Web site (described in the following section). To configure your newsreader program, ask your Internet Service Provider (ISP) for the name of its *news server,* the program that stores newsgroup postings for you to download.

Deja.com and Usenet Indexers

Usenet has been around almost since the beginning of the Internet and is a bit old and creaky. Deja.com, at `www.deja.com`, has done much to bring Usenet into the modern Web era. The Web site has indexed Usenet articles since 1995. You can use Deja.com to

✦ Search for articles by keywords

✦ Look for newsgroups of interest

✦ Read newsgroup articles

✦ Send e-mail to an article's author

✦ Post a reply article to something you read

✦ Post a newsgroup article on a new topic

Many of the World Wide Web search sites described in Part VII index newsgroups as well, although none is as comprehensive as Deja.com. *See also* "Reading Newsgroups with Deja.com," later in this part.

Deja.com is a great place to find answers to problems you may be having with your computer and its software. You can find a newsgroup for almost every system out there, including ones that are obsolete. Try a search string specific to your problem; for example, search on "`ColorZorchWriter streaked output Windows 98.`"

> Watch out what you post on Usenet newsgroups because anyone can find your posts later by using Deja.com! A simple search for your name displays your e-mail address and a list of every message you've posted, at least since 1995.

If you include your home address, phone number, kids' names, political opinions, dating preferences, personal fantasies, or whatever in any message, that information also is easily retrieved. You have been warned.

Frequently Asked Questions (FAQs)

Many newsgroups periodically post a list of frequently asked questions and their answers, or *FAQs*. They hope that you read the FAQ before posting a message they have answered a dozen times before, and you should.

MIT collects FAQs from all over Usenet, creating, in effect, an online encyclopedia with the latest information on a vast array of topics that is accessible with your Web browser or via FTP, at this URL:

`ftp://rtfm.mit.edu/pub/usenet-by-hierarchy`

(The acronym `rtfm` *could* stand for Reference The FAQ Masters.) Also try `www.faq.org`.

FAQs are usually quite authoritative, although sometimes they're just opinion. Reader beware!

Newsgroup Names

Usenet newsgroups have multipart names separated by dots, such as `comp.dcom.fax`, a data communication discussion group about fax machines. Related groups have related names. Groups about data communication, for example, all start with `comp.dcom`. The first part of a newsgroup name is its *hierarchy*.

In e-mail addresses and Internet host names, the top-level component (`edu`, for example) is on the *right*. In newsgroup names, the top-level component is on the *left*.

The most popular Usenet newsgroup hierarchies are

comp	Computer-related topics; lots of meaty discussions
sci	Science-related topics; also meaty
rec	Recreational groups about sports, hobbies, the arts, and other fun endeavors
soc	Social groups, both social interests and plain socializing
news	Topics having to do with the Usenet newsgroup system itself; a few newsgroups with valuable general announcements — otherwise, not very interesting
misc	Miscellaneous topics that don't fit anywhere else
talk	Long arguments, frequently political
alt	Semiofficial "alternate" to the preceding newsgroup hierarchies (which are often called "the big seven"); alt groups range from the extremely useful to the totally weird

Regional, organizational, and national hierarchies also exist:

ne	New England
ny	New York
uk	United Kingdom
ibm	IBM

Many hierarchies serve languages other than English; Zum Beispiel (for example):

de	German
es	Spanish
fj	Japanese
fr	French

New hierarchies are being started all the time. Lewis S. Eisen maintains a master list of Usenet hierarchies (567, at last count), at www.magma.ca/~leisen/mlnh.com.

 You can also click the Browse Groups button at Deja.com to review available newsgroups. *See also* "Deja.com and Usenet Indexers," at the beginning of this part.

Newsgroup Netiquette

The e-mail etiquette rules listed in the "Electronic etiquette" section, in Part III, apply even more to newsgroup articles because *many* more people read newsgroups. Here are some other suggestions:

✦ Don't post to the whole group a follow-up intended solely for the author of the original article. Instead, reply via e-mail.

✦ Be sure that each article is appropriate for the group to which you post it.

✦ Don't post a message saying that another message — a spam ad, for example — is inappropriate. The poster probably knows and doesn't care. The first message wasted enough of everyone's time: Your response would waste more. Silence is the best answer.

✦ Never criticize someone else's spelling or grammar.

✦ Make your subject line as meaningful as possible. If your reply is tangential to an article, change the subject line to reflect the new topic.

✦ When you're asking a question, use a question mark:

```
Subject: Meaning of Life?
```

not

```
Subject: Meaning of Life
```

✦ Don't post a 2-line follow-up that quotes an entire 100-line article. Edit out most of the quoted material.

✦ Don't *cross-post* (that is, post the same article to multiple newsgroups) unless you have a really good reason. Be especially careful when you're replying to multiple cross-posted messages; your response may be cross-posted too.

✦ Watch out for *trolls,* messages calculated to provoke a storm of replies. Not every stupid comment needs a response.

✦ Most groups periodically post a list of Frequently Asked Questions (or *FAQs*). Read the FAQ before asking a question. **See also** "Frequently Asked Questions (FAQs)," earlier in this part.

Here are classic messages you should never post:

✦ "I saw something in a book once, but I don't have it here. I think it said. . . ."

✦ "You shouldn't post that kind of message in `alt.foo.bar`."

✦ "I don't have time to read this group. Please just e-mail me the answer."

✦ "Only an <expletive deleted> could possibly think that. . . ."

✦ "This message isn't really about sex, but now that I've got your interest. . . ."

✦ "<large corporation> has offered $245 to each person who replies to this message, so pass it along. . . ."

✦ "Here's how to make a lot of money fast. . . ."

Posting Your First Article

Standard Usenet dogma is to read a group for a few weeks before posting anything. It's still good advice, although Internet newbies generally aren't big on delayed gratification. Here are some tips on your first posting:

✦ Pick a newsgroup whose subject is one you know something about.

✦ Read the FAQ before you post.

✦ Reply to an article with specific information you know firsthand or that you can cite in a reference and that is relevant to the topic being discussed.

✦ Read the entire preceding *thread* (a series of replies to the original article and replies to those replies) to make sure that your point hasn't been raised already.

✦ Edit included text from the original article to the bare minimum.

✦ Keep your reply short, clear, and to the point.

✦ Have your facts straight. Your article should contain more than your opinion.

✦ Check your spelling and grammar.

✦ Stay calm. Don't be inflammatory, use foul language, or call people names.

✦ Avoid Netisms, such as ROFL ("rolling on floor laughing"). If necessary, use — at most — one smiley :-). ***See also*** "Abbreviations and Acronyms" in Part III.

✦ Use a local hierarchy for stuff of regional interest. The whole planet does not need to hear about your school's bake sale.

✦ Edit the follow-up newsgroup list to one newsgroup.

✦ Save your message overnight, and reread it before posting.

Some newsgroups are *moderated,* which means that

✦ Articles are not posted directly as news. Instead, they're e-mailed to a person or program who posts the article only if he, she, or it feels that it's appropriate to the group.

✦ Moderators, because they're unpaid volunteers, do not process items instantaneously, so it can take a day or two for items to be processed. Don't nag.

✦ If you post an article for a moderated group, the news-posting software mails your item to the moderator automatically.

✦ If your article doesn't appear and you really don't know why, post a polite inquiry to the same group.

Remember that Usenet is a public forum. Everything you say there can be read by anyone, anywhere in the world. Worse, every word you post is carefully indexed and archived. **See also** "Deja.com and Usenet Indexers," at the beginning of this part.

To reply to a message via e-mail, find the person's e-mail address in the article and copy it into the To field of your favorite e-mail program.

Many people disguise their return address in Usenet postings to foil spammers. For example, you may see

`use_my_first_name at iecc dot com`

You would translate this as `arnold@iecc.com`.

Ramping Up Your Own Newsgroup

You can start your own newsgroup, although the process is not for the fainthearted. Most hierarchies have a newsgroup — for example, `news.groups` or `alt.config` — in which proposals for new groups are presented, discussed, and disposed of, by vote or consensus.

Here are some things you have to do if you want to start a new newsgroup:

✦ Understand Usenet's and your hierarchy's culture.

✦ Think about who will want to join your group and how you will let them know about it.

✦ Spend some time reading `news.groups` and `alt.config`.

✦ Make sure that a suitable group doesn't already exist.

✦ Pick the right hierarchy and name for your group. The folks who run Usenet groups are really picky about names.

✦ Write a strong justification.

✦ Find as many allies as possible.

✦ Be tenacious.

For more information about starting your own group, see the newsgroup `news.groups.questions` or visit this Web page:

`www.geocities.com/ResearchTriangle/Lab/6882/ncreate.html`

You can start your own discussion group without much fuss at a number of portal sites on the Web. For example, to set up a discussion group at Deja.com (on the Web at `www.deja.com`), click on My Deja and register if you haven't already done so. Then click the Communities link, click the Create New Community link, and fill out the form you see.

You can also conduct online discussions on mailing lists (*see* Part V to find out how to set up a mailing list for free).

Reading Newsgroups with America Online

To subscribe to and read newsgroups by using America Online 5.0, follow these steps:

Internet

1. Choose Internet⇨Newsgroups from the toolbar or type **newsgroups** in the Keyword box. You see the Newsgroups window. The first time you use this command, AOL may display instructions for filtering junk messages in newsgroups.

Add
Newsgroups

2. Subscribe to newsgroups by clicking the Add Newsgroups button in the Newsgroups window. Choose the hierarchy the group belongs to (the first part of the newsgroup name), and continue specifying parts of the name. Click Subscribe when you find the group you want.

Read My
Newsgroups

3. Click the Read My Newsgroups icon in the Newsgroups window. You see your personalized list of newsgroups. AOL starts you out with a handful of groups (including `news.announce.newusers`, `news.answers`, and `news.groups.reviews`) and some AOL help groups.

4. Double-click the group you want to read. You see a list of threads in your selected newsgroup. Double-click a thread to start reading it.

TIP

In the Newsgroups window, click the Set Preferences button and then click the Filtering tab on the window that appears. You can choose to filter out (skip viewing) classes of messages based on size, excessive cross-posting, specific text in the subject, or postings by a specific author.

Reading Newsgroups with Deja.com

Deja.com updates its site from time to time, so the details described in this section may change.

Searching Deja.com

The traditional way to read Usenet is to go to a newsgroup and read the recent messages posted there. With tens of thousands of newsgroups, this method has become very inefficient. Deja.com lets you search *all* newsgroups by content:

1. Open your browser and go to www.deja.com.

2. In the Quick Search part of the Web page, make sure that Discussions is selected, type some key words in the search box, and click Search.

You see a list of newsgroups that include many articles with those keywords, followed by a list of specific articles. You can sort this list by date, subject, newsgroup, or author; click the link at the top of each column.

3. Click an article to read it. To see other articles on the same topic, click the Thread link in the article window. To read other postings in the same newsgroup, click the Forum thread. To return to the last search list, click Back to Search Results (or your browser's Back button).

4. To save an article, choose File⇨Save as in your browser.

If you don't find what you want in the search results, click Next Messages to see more articles or change your key words in the search box and click Find. ***See also*** "Search strategies," in Part VII.

When you first do a search, Deja.com looks at only the articles posted in the past month or so. If you want older articles, look for the search box at the bottom of the list of articles, change Recent to Past or All messages, and click Find.

Using Deja.com as a newsreader

1. Start your browser, go to www.deja.com, and click the My Deja link near the upper-left corner of the Deja.com window.

If you're a Deja.com member, you see your personalized list of *forums,* what Deja.com calls *newsgroups.* If you're not a member, you're asked to register. Do so.

2. Click the button to the left of the forum you want to peruse and click Read. You see a list of messages in your selected newsgroup. Click a message to read it. To see other messages on the same topic, click View Thread in the upper-right part of the message window.

3. To subscribe to a newsgroup, click the Subscribe to a New Forum link on the My Deja Web page. If you know the name of the group, type it in the search box. If not, type some key words related to your interests. For example, if you enter the keywords `inline skates`, Deja.com offers you

```
rec.sport.skating.inline
rec.sport.skating.ice.recreational
rec.sport.skating.racing
```

4. Click the Subscribe button next to the group you want.

5. To unsubscribe, click the Unsubscribe button next to the group you're bored with.

Replying to articles

To reply to a message via e-mail, find the person's e-mail address in the article and copy it in the To field of your favorite e-mail program.

To post an article following up on a message, click the Post Reply link. On the Quick Post Message page, edit the quoted article to a reasonable size and add your response. You can also edit the list of newsgroups to which your article is posted. Click Preview to see what your message will look like, and click Send when it's ready for public viewing. If you haven't registered with Deja.com, Deja.com sends you e-mail asking for confirmation before posting your message.

The Power Post link offers you more options, including sending a copy of your posting to the originator.

Deja.com provides check boxes in which you can specify whether your article should be spell checked and whether you want a copy of your response e-mailed to you. Both are good ideas.

Posting a new article

To post a new message to a newsgroup, display an article in the newsgroup and then click the Post Reply link. On the Quick Post Message page, replace the text in the Subject box with your new title. *See also* "Newsgroup Netiquette," earlier in this part. Type the message in the text box. You can also edit the list of newsgroups to which your article is posted. Click the Preview button, and reread your message carefully and fix it up. When it's perfect, click the Send button.

Reading Newsgroups with Netscape Newsgroup

To use the Netscape Newsgroup program that comes with Netscape Communicator 4.7, choose Communicator⇨Newsgroups from the menu. In the Netscape Newsgroup window that appears, you see your mail folders and news servers listed down the left side of the window.

To tell Netscape the name of your ISP's news server, choose File⇨Subscribe. On the Subscribe to Newsgroups window that appears, click the Add Server button, choose to add an NNTP news server, and fill in the name of the news server. In the Subscribe to Newsgroups window, you can also view a list of the newsgroups that your ISP's news server stores and choose those to which you want to subscribe. Downloading the entire list of newsgroups the first time you connect to a news server can take a long time — several minutes.

The newsgroups you're subscribed to appear on the folder list on the left side of the Netscape Newsgroup window, indented below the news server name. To read a newsgroup, click it to download the headers of the new messages. The messages in that newsgroup appear in the upper-right part of the window, arranged by thread (topic). Click a message to display its text in the lower-right part of the window.

To reply to a message by e-mail to its author, right-click the Reply icon on the toolbar and choose To Sender Only from the menu that appears. To post a response to the newsgroup, just click Reply. To post a message on a new topic, click the New Msg icon on the tool-bar. In all three cases, you see a Composition window in which you can type your message and click Send to e-mail your message or post it to the newsgroup.

Reading Newsgroups with Outlook Express

Outlook Express, the e-mail program that comes with Internet Explorer and Windows 98, also works as a newsreader. In the Outlook Express window, choose Go⇨News from the menu. The first time, Outlook Express may ask whether you want it to be your default newsreader. Then Outlook Express lists your subscribed newsgroups in the upper-right part of its window. Your news server should appear at the bottom of the list of your e-mail folders. (If it doesn't, or if you need to change the address of your news server, choose Tools⇨Accounts from the menu.)

To subscribe to newsgroups, click the Newsgroups icon on the toolbar and then select from the immense alphabetical list of newsgroups. To read a newsgroup, double-click it on the list of your subscribed newsgroups in the upper-right part of the Outlook Express window: The newsgroup list moves to the left part of the window and a list of messages appears in the upper-right area.

To read a message, click it on the list of messages. The text of the message appears in the lower-right part of the Outlook Express window. You can reply privately to the author by clicking the Reply to Author icon on the toolbar or post a response to the newsgroup by clicking Reply to Group. To post a message on a new topic, click the Compose Message icon. In all three cases, you see a composition window: Type your message and click the Post button.

Reading Newsgroups with Other Newsreader Programs

Many powerful programs are written only to read Usenet newsgroups. Free Agent is a free newsreader for Windows from Forté, Inc. You can use your Web browser to download a copy from www.forteinc.com. If you like Free Agent, you may also look at its inexpensive, commercial, larger sibling, named Agent.

A comparable program for Macintosh users is John Norstad's Newswatcher, available from www.shareware.com or www.tucows.com.

Part V

Mailing Lists

An e-mail *mailing list* offers a way for people with a shared interest to send messages to each other and hold a group conversation. Mailing lists differ from newsgroups in that a separate copy of the mailing list message is e-mailed to each recipient on the list.

Mailing lists are generally smaller and more intimate than newsgroups. Lists can be very specific, tend to be less raucous, and are less infested with spam.

Imagine a mailing list that would keep you up-to-date in an area vital to your work or one that would let you exchange views with people who share your fondest passions. That list probably already exists. We give you hints on how to find it and how to start it if it doesn't exist.

Remember: Because mailing-list messages arrive via e-mail and all transactions use e-mail, you can participate regardless of which kind of Internet service you have. You can even use the free e-mail services described in Part III.

In this part . . .

- ✔ Addresses used with mailing lists
- ✔ Finding a mailing list
- ✔ Getting on and off a mailing list
- ✔ Open and closed mailing lists
- ✔ Receiving mailing-list messages
- ✔ Sending messages to a mailing list
- ✔ Sending special requests to mailing lists
- ✔ Starting your own mailing list
- ✔ Using filters

Addresses Used with Mailing Lists

Each mailing list has its own e-mail address; on most lists, anything sent to that address is remailed to all the people on the list. People on the list respond to messages and create a running conversation. Some lists are *moderated,* which means that a reviewer (moderator) skims messages and decides which to send out.

Every mailing list, in fact, has *two* e-mail addresses:

♦ *List address:* Messages sent to this address are forwarded to all the people who subscribe to the list.

♦ *Administrative address:* Messages sent to this address are read by only the list's owner. Use this address for messages about subscribing and unsubscribing. Messages to the administrative address are often processed entirely by a computer, called a *mailing list server, list server,* or *MLM* (mailing list manager). In that case, you have to type your message in a specific format, as described throughout this part.

Always send e-mail to the administrative address, not to the list address, for matters such as subscribing or unsubscribing from the list. If you use the list address, everyone on the list sees your request *except* for the person or computer that needs to act on it. Proper use of the administrative address is probably the most important thing you need to know about using mailing lists.

You can usually figure out the administrative address if you know the list address:

♦ **Manually maintained lists:** Add **-request** to the list address. If a manual list is named `unicycles@blivet.com`, for example, the administrative address is almost certainly `unicycles-request@blivet.com`.

♦ **Automatically-maintained lists:** The request address is usually the name of the type of list server program at the host where the list is maintained. Look for the server name in a message header to determine how a list is maintained. The most common list server programs are ListProc, LISTSERV, Mailbase, Lyris, and Majordomo.

♦ **Web-based lists:** A number of companies run Web sites that host mailing lists for free in exchange for placing an ad at the end of each message. These firms accept administrative requests at their Web site, and some allow you to read list messages and archives there, too. Popular Web-based list servers include

```
www.coollist.com
www.egroups.com
www.onelist.com
www.topica.com
```

Some mailing list servers don't care whether your administrative request is in upper- or lowercase — others may. We show all commands in uppercase, which generally works with all servers.

Finding a Mailing List

Here are three excellent Web sites that maintain extensive indexes to mailing lists:

```
www.liszt.com
catalog.com/vivian/interest-group-search.html
paml.taronga.com
```

In many cases, the best way to find out about mailing lists is to ask colleagues and friends who share your interests. Many lists are informally maintained and are not indexed anywhere.

Getting On and Off a Mailing List

The way you get on or off a mailing list — subscribing and unsubscribing — depends on how the list is maintained. Subscribing to a mailing list (unlike subscribing to a magazine) is almost always free.

Lists maintained manually

Send a mail message (such as "Please add me to the unicycles list" or "Please remove me from the unicycles list") to the request address. Keep these tips in mind:

✦ Include your real name and complete e-mail address so that the poor list owner doesn't have to pick through your e-mail header.

✦ Because the messages are read by humans, no fixed form is required.

✦ Be patient. The person maintaining the list is probably a volunteer and may have a life — or be trying to get one.

Lists maintained automatically

To join a list, send an e-mail message to its administrative address with no subject and the following line as the body of the message:

SUBSCRIBE *listname your-name*

Replace *listname* with the name of the mailing list, and *your-name* with your actual name. You don't have to include your e-mail address because it's automatically included as your message's return address. For example, William Clinton would type the following line to subscribe to the leader_support mailing list:

```
SUBSCRIBE leader_support William J. Clinton
```

+ For Mailbase lists, replace SUBSCRIBE with JOIN.

+ For Majordomo lists, don't include your name.

To get off a list, send e-mail to its administrative address with no subject and the following line as the body of the message:

```
UNSUBSCRIBE listname
```

The command SIGNOFF works with most mailing lists, too.

For Mailbase lists, replace UNSUBSCRIBE with LEAVE.

When you're subscribing to a list, be sure to send your message from the computer to which you want list messages mailed. The administrator of the list uses your message's return address as the address he adds to the mailing list.

When you first subscribe to a list, you generally receive a welcome message via e-mail. Keep this message! You may want to keep a file of these messages because they tell you what type of server is being used and how to unsubscribe.

Remember: Be sure to send requests to get on and off the list to the administrative address, not to the list itself.

Many list servers e-mail you back for confirmation before processing your request. If you plan to unsubscribe from a bunch of lists before going on vacation — a good idea to keep your mailbox from overflowing — be sure to allow enough time to receive and return the confirmation requests.

Web-based lists

You usually join or leave Web-based lists by going to the list company's Web site, although you can often use e-mail too. Most services ask you to append "-subscribe" or "-unsubscribe" (without the quotes) to the list name. For example, send e-mail to gerbils-subscribe@onelist.com to join the gerbils list at ONElist.

Open and Closed Mailing Lists

Most mailing lists are *open,* which means that anyone can send a message to the list. Some lists, however, are closed and accept

messages only from subscribers. Other lists accept members by
invitation only.

If you belong to a closed list and your e-mail address changes, you
must let the list managers know so that they can update their
database.

Receiving Digested Mailing Lists

As soon as you join a list, you automatically receive all messages
from the list along with the rest of your mail.

Some lists are available in digest form with all the day's messages
combined in a table of contents. To get the digest form, send an
e-mail message to the list's administrative address with no subject
and one of the following lines as the body of the message:

Server	Message
ListProc	SET *listname* MAIL DIGEST
LISTSERV	SET *listname* DIGEST
Majordomo	SUBSCRIBE *listname*-digest, UNSUBSCRIBE *listname*

To undo the digest request, send one of the following messages:

Server	Message
ListProc	SET *listname* MAIL ACK
LISTSERV	SET *listname* MAIL
Majordomo	UNSUBSCRIBE *listname*-digest, SUBSCRIBE *listname*

Sending Messages to a Mailing List

To send a message to a mailing list, just e-mail it to the list's address.
The message is automatically distributed to the list's members.

If you respond to a message with your mail program's Reply button,
check to see — before you click Send — whether your reply will be
sent to the list address. Edit out the list address if you're replying to
only the message's author.

Some lists are moderated — in other words, a human being screens
messages before sending them out to everybody else, which can
delay messages by as much as a day or two.

Mail servers usually send you copies of your own messages to confirm that they were received.

Special Requests to Mailing Lists

Depending on which list server manages a list, various other commands may be available.

Archives: Many mailing lists store their messages for later reference. To find out where these archives are kept, send the following message to the administrative address:

```
INDEX listname
```

Some lists make their archives available on a Web site: Read the message you received when you joined the list.

Subscriber list: To get a list of (almost) all the people who subscribe to a list, send one of the following messages to the administrative address:

Server	Message
ListProc	RECIPIENTS *listname*
LISTSERV	REVIEW *listname* BY NAME F=MAIL
Mailbase	REVIEW *listname*
Mailserve	SEND/LIST *listname*
Majordomo	WHO *listname*

Privacy: ListProc and LISTSERV mail servers don't give out your name as just described if you send one of the following messages to the administrative address:

Server	Message
ListProc	SET *listname* CONCEAL YES
LISTSERV	SET *listname* CONCEAL

To unconceal yourself:

Server	Message
ListProc	SET *listname* CONCEAL NO
LISTSERV	SET *listname* NOCONCEAL

Going on vacation: To stop messages from a list temporarily:

Server	Message
ListProc	SET *listname* MAIL POSTPONE
LISTSERV	SET *listname* NOMAIL

To resume temporarily stopped messages:

Server	Message
ListProc servers	SET *listname* MAIL ACK
	or SET *listname* MAIL NOACK
	or SET *listname* MAIL DIGEST
LISTSERV servers	SET *listname* MAIL

List managers can do many more tricks. For a list of them, visit lawwww.cwru.edu/cwrulaw/faculty/milles/mailser.html or check out our own mailing list page, at lists.gurus.com.

Starting Your Own Mailing List

Here are some tips for starting a new mailing list:

✦ Before you start a new list, *see* "Finding a Mailing List," earlier in this part, to see whether a list that meets your needs already exists.

✦ You can start a simple manual list with nothing more than an e-mail program that supports distribution lists. When a message comes in, just forward it to the distribution list.

✦ Put manual distribution lists in the Bcc address field if you don't want every message to include all recipients' names in the header. You can put your own address in the To field, if you want.

✦ You will soon tire of administering your list manually. Some Internet Service Providers let you use their list server, or use one of the ad-supported, Web-based services listed at the beginning of this part. If someone in your group has a university affiliation, that person may be able to have the list maintained there for free.

✦ Creating a Web page for your list makes it easy to find by using the Internet's search engines. *See* the section in Part IX about creating your own web home page.

✦ For public lists, inform the Web sites listed under "Finding a Mailing List," earlier in this part. Each site has instructions for adding your new mailing list to their collections.

Using Filters

Joining even one mailing list can overwhelm your e-mail inbox. Some e-mail programs can sort through your incoming mail and put mailing list messages in special mailboxes or folders that you can look at when you have time.

If you use Eudora, choose Tools⇨Filters or Special⇨Filters, click New, and copy the To line from a mailing list message and paste it into the contains box. Then specify the mailbox where you want the messages transferred under Actions.

If you use Outlook Express, choose Tools⇨Inbox Assistant, click Add, and copy the To line from a mailing list and paste it in the To box in the Properties window. Then click Moved to and specify the folder where you want the messages moved.

Part VI

The World Wide Web

The *World Wide Web* is a system that uses the Internet to link vast quantities of information all over the world. At times, the Web resembles a library, newspaper, bulletin board, and telephone directory — all on a global scale. "The vision I have for the Web," says its inventor, Tim Berners-Lee, "is about anything being potentially connected to anything." Still very much a work in progress, the Web is destined to become the primary repository of human culture. Already the Web has become the first place to look for answers to almost any question under the sun and beyond.

In this part . . .

- ✔ Getting started with the Web
- ✔ Finding your way around
- ✔ Monitoring kids, porn, and the Web
- ✔ Using plug-ins, helper applications, and ActiveX controls
- ✔ Considering privacy, security, and cookies
- ✔ Troubleshooting problems and error messages
- ✔ Understanding Uniform Resource Locators (URLs)
- ✔ Using America Online to browse the Web
- ✔ Using Internet Explorer to browse the Web
- ✔ Using Lynx to browse the Web
- ✔ Using Netscape Navigator to browse the Web

ABCs of the Web

To start using the World Wide Web, all you need is an Internet connection and a program called a Web browser. A *Web browser* displays, as individual pages on your computer screen, the various types of information found on the Web and lets you follow the connections — called *hypertext links* — built-in to Web pages.

Here are some basic concepts:

+ **Hypertext:** A type of electronic document that contains pointers to other documents. These links appear in a distinct color or are highlighted when the document is displayed by your browser. When you click a hypertext link, your Web browser displays the document to which the link points, if the document is available.

+ **Uniform Resource Locator (URL):** The standard format used for hypertext links on the Internet; `http://net.gurus.com`, for example. They're also called *URIs* (for Universal Resource Identifiers) which also encompass links to things like subparts of e-mail messages; in fact, the inventor of the Web, Tim Berners-Lee, prefers this term. *See also* "Uniform Resource Locators (URLs)," later in this part.

+ **Web site:** A collection of Web pages devoted to a single topic or organization.

+ **Webmaster:** The person in charge of a Web site.

+ **Surfing:** The art and vice of bouncing from Web page to Web page in search of whatever.

Common Web browsers and the computer systems for which they're available include

+ **Netscape Navigator:** Developed by Netscape Communications Corporation, Navigator is available for the Macintosh, Microsoft Windows, Linux, and UNIX. A free version is available at `home.netscape.com`. Navigator comes as part of Netscape Communicator, a suite of programs that includes a powerful HTML editor for making your own Web pages, an e-mail program named Messenger, and a newsreader named Netscape Newsgroups. *See also* "Creating your own Web home page," in Part IX.

+ **Internet Explorer:** The Microsoft browser comes with new Macs and with Microsoft Windows, though the U.S. Department of Justice is challenging this practice on antitrust grounds. Internet Explorer is also available for free at `www.microsoft.com`.

+ **Lynx:** A text-only browser available on UNIX systems and from Internet providers with UNIX shell accounts. Because Lynx displays only the text portion of Web documents, it's handy for people with special needs or older computers that cannot keep up with graphical browsers.

+ **America Online (AOL):** AOL comes with Internet Explorer, though you can use Netscape, if you prefer.

Windows 98 even lets you choose a Web-style desktop that makes your computer behave like one big Web page. Later in this part of the book, we tell you about Netscape Navigator 4.7, Internet Explorer 5, Lynx, and the AOL 5.0 adaptation of Internet Explorer.

Web browsers can handle most, but not all, types of information found on the Net. You can add software called *plug-ins* and *ActiveX controls,* which extend your browser's capabilities. (*See* "Plug-Ins, Helper Programs, and ActiveX Controls," later in this part.)

Finding Your Way around the Web

The Web displays pages of information with hypertext links that take you to other pages. Browsers usually **highlight the links** to make them easy to spot, by using a different color for the item and underlining it. Some links are just areas you click inside a graphics image or photograph. Here are some link tips:

+ On a system that uses windows and a mouse, such as Internet Explorer or Netscape Navigator, use the mouse to click the link. If the page doesn't fit onscreen, click the scroll bar to scroll up and down.

+ On a text system, such as Lynx, press the up- and down-arrow keys to move the cursor to the link you want and then press Enter.

+ Many mail programs, including Eudora, automatically detect and highlight URLs in e-mail messages. You can activate these links by just clicking them in the mail program.

You can bring up a page on your browser in ways other than following a link:

+ Select a page from your browser's list of sites whose addresses you saved (*bookmarks* or *favorites*).

+ Type a URL in the address field on your browser's screen. *See also* "Uniform Resource Locators (URLs)," later in this part.

♦ If you have the page stored as a file on a disk or CD-ROM on your computer, most browsers let you open it by choosing the File⇨Open command.

When you save a Web page (by choosing the File⇨Save As command), browsers give you a choice of text or source (HTML) format. Pick Source or HTML format if you plan to view the page later with your browser. A saved page usually doesn't include all the graphics that appear on the page — you get only the text.

Your browser can link to items other than Web pages:

♦ **File items containing text, pictures, movies, or sound:** If your Web browser can handle the file, the browser displays or plays the file. If not, the browser just tells you about the file or asks which program to use to open it.

♦ **Search query items that let you type one or more key words:** A Web page displays the results of your search.

♦ **Forms you fill out:** The answers are sent as a long URL when you click Done, Submit, or a similar button on the form.

♦ **Small computer programs named *Java applets:*** You download and run them on your computer. (*See also* Part IX.)

Some Web browsers, including Netscape and Internet Explorer, can also access older Internet information systems, such as FTP, Gopher, Archie, and WAIS databases. (*See also* Part X.)

Another way of accessing information on the Web is by using *channels.* Channels allow a Web site to deliver content to your computer whenever the site has new information for you. You can read the information later.

Kids, Porn, and the Web

The World Wide Web abounds in great resources for kids. Many kids have their own home pages, and cyberspace is filled with scanned artwork of the kind that once adorned refrigerator doors. You can find a collection of Web resources at our kids' page, at net.gurus. com/kids.

Though pornography and other dangerous material on the Internet has been overhyped, more than enough of it is available to fill anyone's hard disk. If you have underage children, you need to control their access to the Internet. You can do it in three main ways: Watch over your kid's shoulder, use filtering (censoring) software, and sign up with an Internet provider that filters out unwanted stuff.

Access supervision

Using this method, you simply don't allow your kid on the Net unless you or an adult you trust are present. If you want, kids can save pages they find and look at them later — offline. Although this method takes a great deal of your time and limits your kids' spontaneity online, it can be very effective and builds family togetherness.

Buying filtering software

Several companies sell software that filters out Web pages that are inappropriate for kids. This kind of software runs on your computer and blocks your kids from seeing inappropriate stuff without restricting your access. Some popular vendors are

✦ **CyberPatrol:** www.cyberpatrol.com

✦ **Net Nanny:** www.netnanny.com

✦ **SafeSurf:** www.safesurf.com

✦ **SurfWatch:** www.surfwatch.com

✦ **Cybersitter:** www.solidoak.com

None of these programs tells you exactly what they filter out; their idea of what's appropriate or inappropriate may not match yours.

Using an online service with built-in filtering

Both America Online and CompuServe help parents limit their kids' access. Although the filtering programs described in the preceding section work adequately if you install and use them properly, your kids probably know more about them than you do. Software that runs at the service-provider level may be more foolproof.

✦ **On AOL:** Click in the keyword box (in the middle of the row of buttons just below the toolbar) or press Ctrl+K, and then type **parental control.**

✦ **On CompuServe:** Click the Go button and type **controls**.

You must set some rules for your kids. Here are a few, based on the America Online guidelines:

✦ Never agree to meet someone in person or call them on the phone without asking a parent first.

✦ Never give out your last name, address, phone number, Social Security number, or the name of your school without asking a parent first.

✦ Never share your login password, even with your best friend.

✦ If someone tells you not to tell your parents about them, tell your parents right away!

✦ If you see anything that makes you feel scared or uncomfortable or if you just aren't sure, ask a parent or teacher.

Ask your kids to give *you* a tour of the Internet. You can find out a great deal by seeing it through their eyes.

Plug-Ins, Helper Programs, and ActiveX Controls

New data formats are being developed all the time to let the Web do new tricks. Though Web browsers resemble Swiss army knives, with tools for opening almost anything, most browsers let you expand their repertoire by adding other software. Three types of software work with browsers:

✦ **Helper programs:** Helper programs work with your browser to run or display files your browser can't understand by itself. These files are displayed in the helper program's window. For example, if you run across an Adobe Acrobat-format file on the Net, Adobe Acrobat Reader can act as a helper program to display the file for you.

✦ **Plug-ins:** These programs attach themselves to your browser and give it more capabilities, such as handling additional types of files. Although plug-ins were invented by Netscape, Internet Explorer can run them, too. Netscape has a catalog of helper applications and plug-ins at home.netscape.com/plugins.

✦ **ActiveX controls:** Internet Explorer can use Netscape plug-ins but pushes a different Microsoft-developed technology, called ActiveX controls. These controls aren't as popular as plug-ins. You can find out more about ActiveX at www.microsoft.com/com/tech/activex.asp.

ActiveX controls present a security risk because they can access and change anything in your computer. Use only ActiveX controls you download from a source you trust.

This section describes a few of the most popular helper programs and plug-ins with the URL of the Web site where you can download the program or plug-in.

ZipMagic (Windows only)

www.mijenix.com/

ZipMagic works with compressed files that are in ZIP format, by making ZIP files look and act just like folders. You can use Windows Explorer to move or copy files into and out of ZIP files — very convenient!

WinZip (Windows only)

www.winzip.com/

WinZip expands most compressed-file formats found on the Internet. The program can also compress files. It's essential for Windows users, unless you already have ZipMagic.

StuffIt Expander and DropStuff with Expander Enhancer (Macintosh)

www.aladdinsys.com/

StuffIt Expander and DropStuff with Expander Enhancer are Macintosh file-expansion and -compression programs. Working together, these programs can handle virtually every compression format found on Macs, UNIX systems, and IBM compatibles. These formats include ZIP (.zip), ARC (.arc), AppleLink (.pkg), gzip (.gz), UNIX Compress (.Z), uuencode (.uu), StuffIt (.sit), and Compact Pro (.cpt) and files encoded in BinHex (.hqx) and MacBinary (.bin) formats. Essential for Macintosh users, StuffIt Expander is also available for Windows.

RealPlayer (formerly RealAudio)

www.real.com/products/player/

RealPlayer lets you listen to and watch live, on-demand audio and video on the Internet over standard modems, effectively turning the Internet into another television band. RealPlayer is free for individual use.

Acrobat Reader

www.adobe.com/prodindex/acrobat/readstep.html

With so many different word processors, page-layout programs, and other types of programs now available, the world needs a standard way to exchange print-quality electronic documents. The Adobe Portable Document Format (.pdf) is widely used for that purpose. To view, navigate, and print .PDF files, you need the free Adobe Acrobat Reader.

Macromedia Shockwave
www.macromedia.com/shockwave/

Many Web sites feature amazing video and audio effects that go beyond what browsers can display. To view these sites, you need a multimedia plug-in; the most popular is Shockwave.

Apple QuickTime
www.apple.com/quicktime

QuickTime is an Apple system that lets you experience animation, music, MIDI, voice, video, and panoramic virtual reality. Its fast-start feature enables you to get started while the file you're displaying is still downloading from the Net. QuickTime runs under Windows as well as on Macs, and you can get it free from Apple.

Privacy, Security, and Cookies

Surfing the Web from your home may feel totally safe and anonymous. It isn't. The messages your browser sends to get information from the Web are often recorded. Web sites can also ask your browser to save (or set) a small lump of information, a *cookie,* that the site can ask for the next time you visit. Also, the messages you send, such as completed forms, can be intercepted by computer vandals and criminals as the messages pass through the network if they aren't encrypted.

This section gives you the scoop on privacy on the Net.

Cookies
Cookies are commonly used to

   ✦ Keep track of how often you visit a site.

   ✦ Save your login name and site password so that you don't have to go through a login procedure every time you visit.

   ✦ Store your billing address and credit card number.

   ✦ Save a user profile so that the site can present information customized to your needs.

Your browser enforces rules to prevent cookie abuse:

   ✦ Cookies are limited in size (4 kilobytes).

   ✦ They can be accessed by only the site that set them.

   ✦ They must have an expiration date.

You can ask your browser to tell you when a Web site wants to set a cookie:

✦ **Netscape Communicator:** Choose <u>E</u>dit⇨P<u>r</u>eferences, click Advanced on the Category list, and then click the <u>W</u>arn me Before Accepting A Cookie option in the Cookies box. (Or is it cookie jar?)

✦ **Internet Explorer:** Choose <u>V</u>iew⇨Internet <u>O</u>ptions, click the Advanced tab, scroll down to the Security heading and the Cookies subheading, and click to put a check in the Prompt Before Accepting Cookies option.

Web sites can track visitors in ways other than the use of cookies. If the lack of Web privacy makes you nervous, visit www.anonymizer.com before you go surfing. It blocks the common ways that sites use to track you.

Secure surfing

Just as strategies exist for preserving privacy while surfing, you can prevent anyone from reading your messages, by *encrypting* them in a secret code. Many sites offer encrypted transactions for form submittals and credit card purchases. These sites typically have URLs starting with https:// (rather than http://) — the *s* stands for *secure.* Your browser indicates when a page offers security. Netscape, for example, shows a broken key or an open padlock in the lower-left corner of its window when the connection is not secure and a whole key or a closed padlock when the connection is secure.

Unfortunately, the United States and other governments have attempted to hobble the use of this technology so that they can read messages that they believe pose a threat to their interests. (***See also*** Part IX.) As a result, browsers have one of three levels of security:

✦ **International 40-bit security:** This level is the only one the United States allowed to be exported until recently. It uses codes so weak that they can be broken by sophisticated amateurs.

✦ **International 56-bit security:** This level is the highest the United States allows to be exported. Its codes are stronger, but can still be broken by governments and organized criminals. (64-bit international security may be authorized soon.)

✦ **U.S. or 128-bit security:** Generally available only in the United States and Canada, this level uses codes that many experts believe are unbreakable.

If you obtained your browser via a free download without answering questions about your citizenship, the browser probably uses one of the weaker international security levels. Your browser's About box tells you which you have. Try to get the U.S. or 128-bit version, if you can. International users can upgrade Netscape to U.S. security using tools available from www.fortify.net.

Problems and Error Messages

Because the Web is so new and is growing so fast, much of the software that makes it work is full of bugs and is often downright user-hostile. This section describes some of the most frequently encountered problems that exasperate new and old Web users, with solutions (or at least explanations).

Displaying a page takes too long

The Web can be slow for a number of reasons:

Problem	Solution
Too many graphics on the page.	You can turn off the display of graphics to speed the loading process. Unfortunately, many pages have links you can see only with graphics turned on.
Modem is too slow.	Upgrade to a faster modem or get cable or DSL access. (See also "Modems," in Part II.)
Noise on the telephone line.	Modems slow down automatically when line quality is poor. Disconnect and redial. If the problem persists, pester your phone company to fix your line.
Busy signal when you're dialing in.	Try surfing at a less popular time or shop for an ISP equipped to handle peak loads.
The site you're visiting is overloaded.	Try later or look for a mirror site that has the same information in a part of the world that is asleep. Australia is a good bet for users in the Americas (and vice versa).

Error message "The server does not have a DNS entry"

DNS stands for *domain name server,* a computer that helps other computers figure out the numerical address of a domain from its name. (A *domain* is the last part of a computer's Internet host name, such as gurus.com or whitehouse.gov.) Your service provider keeps a list of common names but asks remote DNS computers for help with names it can't find.

✦ If you typed the URL from a printed source, for example, make sure that you typed it exactly as it was printed.

✦ Be aware that printed sources sometimes transcribe URLs incorrectly. They may, for example, add a hyphen or space at the end of a line, fail to include a tilde (~) character, or spell out the word *dot:* gurus-dot-com rather than gurus.com.

✦ If you clicked a hypertext link or you're sure that you typed the URL correctly, wait a few seconds and try again. Because browsers often don't leave enough time for the name-lookup message to get to the DNS and return, a second try to the same URL often works.

✦ Try typing the URL you want in an Internet search engine, perhaps with additional keywords. *See also* "Directories, Search Engines, and Portals," in Part VII.

Error message "www.bigsite.com has refused your connection" or "Broken pipe"

The Web found the page you were looking for but didn't get back the data in time. It usually means that the site's computer server is down or overloaded or the Web itself is congested. Try again later.

Error message "404 File Not Found"

The good news is that the DNS found the computer associated with the URL you selected. The bad news is that the data file specified in your URL — the stuff after the first single slash — doesn't match what is now on that computer.

If you typed the URL from a printed source, make sure that you typed it exactly as it was printed, including capitalization and the funny tilde (~) character; watch out for the hyphen at the end of a printed line, though. That hyphen may or may not be part of the URL.

If you clicked a hypertext link or you're sure that you typed the URL correctly, the data on the site may have been reorganized. Try "walking up" the URL by deleting the portion to the right of the last slash character, and then the next-to-last slash character, and so on. If you get a File Not Found message when you try this address, for example:

```
world.std.com/~reinhold/pubs/mathmovies/
```

try this one instead:

```
world.std.com/~reinhold/pubs/
```

Then try this one:

`world.std.com/~reinhold/`

or even this one:

`world.std.com/`

At one of these levels, you may find a hint about where the file you seek can be found.

You can also use a search engine. Include in the query box both the filename or topic you seek and the domain name. In the preceding example, you would search for `world.std.com` and `mathmovies`.

Some Web sites offer information on pages with temporary URLs. If you add those pages to your browser's bookmark or favorites list, the pages may not be there when you go back to them. If that happens, go to the site's main page and look for your information again.

For example, if you search for the movie *Star Wars* in the Internet Movie Database (at `www.imdb.com`) and save its page as a bookmark, the URL may be stored as `us.imdb.com/cache/title-exact/108972` at the time you create it. Unfortunately, if you visit the IMDB later, that URL may not work. Because many Web sites create Web pages from information in databases, the information and the pages are different every time you visit the site.

Your browser keeps crashing

This problem is a common one, unfortunately, as software vendors rush to get the latest version of their browsers to market. Make sure that your computer has enough memory — 32MB is minimum, 64MB is recommended — and that you have the latest released (not beta) versions of all the required software.

Uniform Resource Locators (URLs)

One of the key advances that Web technology brought to the Internet is the Uniform Resource Locator, or URL, for short. *URLs* provide a single, standardized way of describing almost any type of information available in cyberspace. The URL tells you which kind of information it is (such as a Web page or an FTP file), which computer it's stored on, and how to find that computer.

URLs are typically long text strings that consist of three parts:

✦ Document access type followed by a colon and two slashes (`://`)

✦ Host name of the computer on which the information is stored

✦ The path to the file that contains the information

In the following example:

`http://world.std.com/~reinhold/papers.html`

the `http` part indicates a hypertext document (a Web page), and `world.std.com` is the host computer on which the Web page is stored. The `/~reinhold/papers.html` part is the file path and name of a file containing a hypertext index to Arnold Reinhold's online papers. *See also* "What's my address?" in Part III for more information about host names.

Be careful to enter URLs exactly as they're written, and be especially careful about uppercase and lowercase letters. Many Internet host computers run UNIX, in which capitalization counts in directory names and filenames. Copy and paste URLs or use bookmarks whenever you can.

Some browsers fill in missing information, such as the `http://` prefix, if you leave it out. They often go further. If you type `hopscotch`, for example, earlier versions of Netscape try to take you to `http://www.hopscotch.com`. (Netscape 4.7 assumes that you want to search the Web for the word *hopscotch*. Choose Edit⇨ Preferences, choose the Navigator Smart Browsing category, and turn off Enable Internet Keywords if you don't like this behavior.)

Common document access types include

✦ **http:** For hypertext (the Web)

✦ **https:** For hypertext with a secure link

✦ **ftp:** For File Transfer Protocol files

✦ **gopher:** For Gopher files

✦ **mailto:** For e-mail addresses

The following list includes other mysterious things you see in URLs:

✦ **.html** or **.htm:** The filename extension for a hypertext document; html stands for HyperText Markup Language, the set of codes used to build Web pages.

✦ **index.html:** The master page of a Web site.

✦ **.txt:** A plain-text document without links or formatting.

✦ **.gif, .jpg, .jpeg,** and **.mpg:** Pictures, graphics, or video.

✦ **.mp3:** Music files. You can even get a Walkman-size unit that accepts and plays these files. (*See also* "Music online," in Part VII.)

✦ **.zip, .sit, .hqx, .gz, .tar,** and **.z:** Filename extensions for files that have been compressed to save downloading time. (**See also** "Uncompressing and decoding retrieved files," in Part VII.)

✦ **.Class:** A Java applet.

✦ **~george:** As suggested by the tilde (~) character, probably a UNIX account belonging to someone with the account name of george.

✦ **www:** Short for World Wide Web.

Most, but not all, Web sites have www at the beginning of their host name. For example, net.gurus.com takes you to the Internet Gurus Web site — a neat site where you can find, among other things, updates to this book.

Using AOL to Browse the Web

The AOL software comes with a built-in Web browser. This section describes Version 5.0 of the America Online software, which is available for download from www.aol.com.

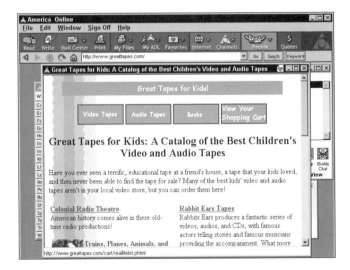

Viewing a Web page

To start the America Online Web browser, sign on to AOL, click the Internet icon on the toolbar, and choose Go to the Web from the menu that appears. Or click in the Keyword box (the wide, white box just below the toolbar), type the URL of the page you want to see (or cut-and-paste to copy it from another window), and press Enter.

Either way, you see the AOL Web browser window and a Web page starts loading. You may have to wait awhile if the page contains many graphics. At the bottom of its window, AOL tells you how things are going.

 If you want to quit waiting, click the Stop icon to the left of the Keyword box.

Changing your home page

When you start the AOL browser (unless you asked for a specific Web page), it displays a home page. Initially, it's the AOL home page, at www.aol.com. You can change the home page location to any Web page:

1. Click the My AOL icon on the toolbar and choose Preferences from the menu that appears. You see the Preferences window.

2. Click the WWW icon. You see the Internet Options window (which is part of Windows, not of the AOL software — at least, it is if you run Windows!).

3. Click the General tab.

4. In the Home Page section, type in the Address box the URL of the Web page where you want AOL to start.

5. Click OK to close the Internet Options window and then close the Preferences window.

Following a hypertext link

Hypertext links in the text of a Web page usually appear underlined and in a distinctive color. Icons or pictures can also be links. Click any link you want to follow. The AOL browser finds and loads the document to which the link points.

When you follow a link, the AOL browser changes the link's color. This feature is handy for keeping track of explored links on a complex page. Of course, you can still click a link that has changed color.

 To go back to the last page you viewed, click the Back button, just below the Read icon on the toolbar.

 If a page doesn't load properly, you can tell AOL to load it again by clicking the Reload button.

 If you click the little button at the right end of the Keyword box, you see a list of URLs you've visited in this session.

Using bookmarks

Typing URLs is a pain. When you find a site you like, you can add it to your Favorite Places list, which is the AOL name for bookmarks:

1. Click the little heart button in the upper-right corner of the window. Or click the Fa_v_orites icon on the toolbar and choose _A_dd Top Window to Favorite Places from the menu that appears.

2. When AOL asks what you want to do, confirm that you want to add the site to your list of favorite places.

3. To go to a Web page on your favorite places list, click the Fa_v_orites icon on the toolbar and choose _F_avorite Places from the menu that appears. You see the Favorite Places window.

4. Double-click an entry in your Favorite Places window to go there.

Pretty soon, your favorite places list starts to get long and unwieldy. Fortunately, you can organize your favorite places. In the Favorite Places window, you can edit and delete items.

Using Internet Explorer to Browse the Web

Internet Explorer (or IE, for short) is the Microsoft Web browser. It comes built-in with new Windows and the Mac computers. This section describes IE Version 5.0.

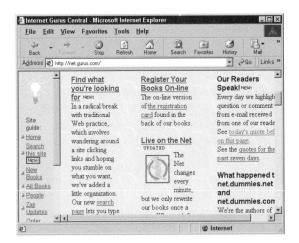

Viewing a Web page

Start Internet Explorer by clicking its icon on the Windows taskbar or desktop or by choosing Start⇨Programs⇨Internet Explorer. When you start Internet Explorer, your starting page is usually the Microsoft home page. To see a Web page whose URL you know, type (or cut-and-paste) the URL directly in the Address box just below the toolbar and then press Enter.

 Internet Explorer tells you, in the lower-left corner of its window, how things are going. You may have to wait awhile. If you want to give up, click the Stop icon.

 If you click the button at the end of the Address box, you see a list of URLs you've visited in the current session.

Changing your home page

You can change the home page location (and your favorite search engine page) by choosing Tools⇨Internet Options to see the Internet Options dialog box. Click the General tab and type the URL in the Home page Address box.

You can alter how Internet Explorer highlights links, too. This capability is handy for black-and-white screens. On the General tab of the Internet Options dialog box, click the Colors button to display the Colors dialog box.

Following a hypertext link

Hypertext links in the text appear in a distinctive color. Icons or pictures can also be links and are typically boxed to distinguish them.

Placing the mouse pointer over a link causes the link's URL to appear in the lower-left corner of the Internet Explorer window. Click any link you want to follow, and Internet Explorer finds and loads the document to which the link points.

 To go back to the last page you viewed, click the Back button, the leftmost icon on the toolbar.

 If a page doesn't load properly, you can tell IE to load it again by clicking the Refresh button.

Playing favorites

When you find a site you like, you can add it to your list of favorites:

1. Choose Favorites⇨Add to Favorites. The Add Favorite dialog box appears.

2. In the Name box, correct the entry to be the way you want it to appear on your list of favorites.

3. Click OK. The site's URL is added to your favorites list.

4. To go to a favorite place, just choose it from the Favorites menu. Or click the Favorites button on the toolbar to display the Favorites window on the left side of the Internet Explorer window, and then choose Web sites from there. (Click the X in the upper-right corner of the Favorites window to close it.)

Pretty soon, your Favorites list starts to get long and unwieldy. Fortunately, you can organize it:

1. Choose Favorites➪Organize Favorites from the menu bar. You see the Organize Favorites window with a list of the items on your Favorites menu.

2. Reorder the entries by dragging them up and down in the list. Delete entries you don't want by selecting them and clicking the Delete button.

3. If you use Windows, the list also includes folders of additional favorite items. Each folder appears on the Favorites menu as a submenu. You can create a folder in which to put favorite entries by clicking Create Folder. On the Mac, choose Favorites➪ New Folder and type a name to add a submenu after an item. Drag into the new folder the items you want to appear on that submenu.

Go for history

You can see each Web site you've visited on your way to where you are now by clicking the History button on the toolbar and looking at the History list that appears on the left side of the Internet Explorer window. Click a Web site on the history list to return to a previous site without hitting the Back button a number of times. Click the X button in the upper-right corner of the History list to make the list disappear.

Although being able to see all the sites you've visited in the past two weeks is handy, remember that anyone else with access to your computer can also see them! To clear the History list, choose Tools➪Internet Options, click the General tab, and then click the Clear History button.

Using Lynx to Browse the Web

Lynx, a Web browser that runs under UNIX, doesn't display graphics, play sounds, or display video clips, although it's extremely fast and great for reading text.

Starting Lynx

To start Lynx, type **lynx** at the UNIX command prompt.

If you know the URL you want to go to, type it after `lynx`, as shown in this example:

```
lynx http://www.hayom.com/mathmovies.html
```

Hypertext links are underlined or highlighted in bold or reverse video. To follow a link:

1. Press the up- or down-arrow keys to select a particular link. Even if the links are on the same line, you still press the up- and down-arrow keys.

2. Press Enter or the right-arrow key when the link you want is highlighted.

Lynx finds the associated file and displays it onscreen.

Browsing with Lynx

Because Lynx is character-based, it cannot display graphics; however, its text-only nature makes it an extremely fast Web browser.

You operate Lynx by typing single-key commands:

Keystroke Command	Description
Down arrow	Highlight next link
Up arrow	Highlight preceding link
Right arrow, Return, or Enter	Go to highlighted link
Left arrow	Go back to preceding link (also exits Help)
+ (or space)	Scroll down to next page
@ms (or b)	Scroll up to preceding page
? (or h)	Get help (go to Help pages)
a	Add current link to bookmark file
d	Download current link
g	Go to user-specified URL or file
k	Show list of key mappings
o	Set your options
p	Print to a file, mail, printer, or other device
q	Quit (capital Q for quick quit)
/	Search for string within current document

(continued)

Keystroke Command	Description
v	View your bookmark file
z	Cancel transfer in progress
Ctrl+H or Backspace	Go to history page
\	Change between normal view and document source

Using Netscape Navigator to Browse the Web

Netscape Communicator comes with Netscape Navigator, the most powerful Web browser (in our humble opinion). Versions are available for Windows, the Mac, and UNIX with X Windows. You can get just the browser functions by downloading only Netscape Navigator. Get either version from the Netscape Web site (www.netscape.com) or a software library, such as TUCOWS (www.tucows.com). This section describes Version 4.7.

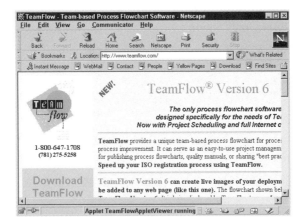

Viewing a Web page

When you start Netscape, it displays your home page, which is usually the Netscape home page at home.netscape.com.

To see a specific Web page whose URL you know, carefully type (or cut-and-paste) the URL directly in the Location or Netsite box that appears below the toolbar. You may have to wait awhile for the Web page to load. Netscape tells you, in the lower-left corner of its window, how things are going.

If you want to give up, click the Stop icon.

Changing your home page

You can change the home page location by choosing Edit⇨ Preferences to see the Preferences dialog box. Click Navigator on the list of categories, make sure that the Navigator Starts With setting is set to Home Page, click in the Home Page Location box, and type a new home page URL. If Netscape now displays the page you want, click the Use Current Page button.

You can also control what colors Netscape uses for displaying links, by choosing Edit⇨Preferences and clicking Colors (it's under Appearance) on the category list.

Following a hypertext link

Hypertext links in the text appear in a distinctive color. Icons or pictures can also be links and may be boxed to distinguish them from regular, nonlinked graphics.

Placing the mouse pointer over a link causes the link's URL to appear in the lower-left corner of the Netscape window. Click any link you want to follow, and Netscape finds and loads the document to which the link points.

When you follow a link, Netscape changes the link's color. This feature is handy when you're exploring a complex page.

 To go back to the last page you viewed, click the Back button, the leftmost icon on the toolbar.

 If a page doesn't load properly, you can tell Netscape to load it again by clicking the Reload button.

Using bookmarks

Typing URLs is a pain. When you find a site you like, you can add it to your list of bookmarks:

✦ To add the current site's URL to your bookmark list, choose Communicator⇨Bookmarks⇨Add Bookmark or press Ctrl+D. Alternatively, drag the little icon to the left of the Location box leftward and drop it on the little icon next to Bookmarks, below the toolbar. (Mac users, just double-click the little icon.)

✦ Drag bookmarks up and down in the list to change their order on the list.

✦ Delete unneeded bookmarks by clicking the entry and pressing Delete.

✦ Edit the name or URL of a bookmark by selecting it and choosing Edit⇨Bookmark Properties.

✦ Choose File⇨New Folder and type a name to add a submenu after an item. Drag into the new folder the items you want to appear on that submenu.

Close the Bookmarks window when you're done editing your bookmarks. Bookmarks aren't saved until you exit from Netscape.

Remembering where you came from

When you're viewing a Web page, you can see the Web sites you've visited on your way to where you are now by choosing Go and looking at the menu that appears. This command lets you return to an earlier site without clicking the Back button a number of times.

Using Netscape plug-ins

Hundreds of Netscape plug-ins are available (*see also* "Plug-Ins, Helper Programs, and ActiveX Controls," earlier in this part). To install a plug-in, follow the instructions that come with the plug-in. If no instructions are available, exit from Netscape and run the installation file you received.

To find and download plug-ins, see the Netscape catalog of helper applications and plug-ins at home.netscape.com/plugins. TUCOWS (at www.tucows.com) also maintains a library of downloadable plug-ins.

Part VII

Finding and Using Resources on the Internet

Need information? The Internet is the first place you should look. Powerful search tools have been developed that can locate data on almost anything. Finding what you need is not quite as easy as typing a question and getting an answer. A little effort is required. In this part, we tell you how to use these tools.

Kids are always asking questions — it took years of education to break *you* of that nasty habit. To benefit the most from this vast, new information resource, get in touch with that childlike curiosity you once had. The World Wide Web never tires of answering questions!

Like to shop? Let your browser do the walking. The Internet brings buyers and sellers together in new ways. You can find anything on the Net. Anything!

In this part . . .

- ✔ **Directories, search engines, and portals**
- ✔ **Free services**
- ✔ **Information sources**
- ✔ **Libraries**
- ✔ **Music online**
- ✔ **Newspapers**
- ✔ **Buying and selling on the Internet**
- ✔ **Software, shareware, and freeware**
- ✔ **Telephone directories**
- ✔ **File unpacking and decoding**
- ✔ **Viruses**

Directories, Search Engines, and Portals

Once, there was a clear distinction between Web directories and search engines. Now, most such sites combine the features of both into a single *portal* site.

Directories

Web *directories* are hierarchical catalogs of the World Wide Web — major topic headings are broken down into smaller areas that are, in turn, broken down further. Web directories work like the card catalog in an old-fashioned, paper-book library.

When you visit a directory site, you see a list of major categories along with selected subcategories. Clicking any category or subcategory displays another page with more entries.

At Yahoo, for example, clicking the Health category and then clicking the subcategory Diseases displays an alphabetized list of more than 50 disease groups — from *allergies* to *vestibular disorders.*

Click a group and you see a list of specific diseases. When you find what you're looking for, just click it.

Engines that search

Several organizations have taken on the formidable task of indexing the entire World Wide Web. Their electronic scouts visit Web sites every few weeks, analyze the text for key words, and follow every hypertext link they find to discover new pages.

The information they gather is available to anyone for free through *search engines,* or computer programs that collect Web page information, index it, and let you search the index.

To use these services:

1. Pick a search engine and go to its Web site.

2. Think of a few words that describe the information you're looking for.

3. Type your search words in the search text box on the search engine's page.

4. Click the Search button or press Enter.

>   The search engine returns a list of Web pages that it thinks match your request. The pages are ranked by how good the match seems to be, with the best match listed first. Unfortunately, the list can contain tens of thousands of pages — way too many to look at.

5. Look over the list. If an item seems interesting, go to that site by clicking the item. (Each item is a hypertext link, of course.)

6. If none of the items listed has what you want, either ask to see more pages that match your search words or alter the search words and try the search again. If the search produces way too many hits, refine your search by typing more words to search for. Click your browser's Back button to get back to the search page, if necessary. *(**See also** "Power searching," later in this part.)*

Portals

Web *portals* combine the best features of directories and search engines and add new features that let you customize what you see at first when you visit them. Popular portal sites include

+ **AltaVista** (www.altavista.com), from Compaq Computer Corp., is our favorite search engine. It even offers free language translation at babelfish.altavsta.com.

+ **Excite** (www.excite.com) reviews many of the sites it lists.

+ **Fast Search** (www.hotbot.com) is from *Wired* magazine.

+ **Google** (www.google.com) ranks relevant Web sites based on the link structure of the Internet itself.

+ **Infoseek** (www.infoseek.com).

+ **Lycos** (www.lycos.com).

+ **Webcrawler** (webcrawler.com).

+ **Yahoo!** (www.yahoo.com) is the best Web portal, we think.

You can find more portal sites at net.gurus.com/search.

Most Internet portal sites let you create a customized home page with news headlines, stock quotes, weather, and sport scores. For the Yahoo version, for example, try my.yahoo.com. The portal sites want you to make them the home page for your browser, and perhaps you should. Pick the portal you like best and see Part VI to find out how.

If you have a Web site, you can ask any of the portals to add your site to their directory and search index. Browse through the directory hierarchy until you find a page where you think a pointer to your Web site belongs. Then look for a button that says something like Add URL. Click that button and you see an online form with instructions for submitting your request.

Directories, search engines, and portals with a twist

So many search and directory sites are available that many have specialized:

+ **Deja** (www.dejanews.com) indexes Usenet newsgroups. (*See* Part IV.)

+ **The Mail Archive** (www.mail-archive.com) indexes selected mailing lists. (*See* Part V.)

+ **MetaCrawler** (www.metacrawler.com) combines answers from several different search engines.

+ **About.com** (www.about.com), formerly The Mining Company, has more than 500 volunteer experts who assemble the best information on the Net about a variety of topics. It's usually worth a visit.

+ **Suite101** (www.suite101.com) is a community-based Best of the Web guide.

+ ***Web rings*** are collections of related sites that agree to link to one another. You can find an indexed list of thousands of them at www.webring.com.

Power searching

Here are some ways to sharpen your search request (these tips work on AltaVista, although most search engines are similar):

+ Capitalize words only when you're sure that they would be stored that way — names of people or places, for example. Search words must match exactly if they have any capitalized letters or accent characters. Lowercase search words match any capitalization.

+ Put double quotation marks (" ") around words you expect to see next to each other. Words connected by punctuation — including URLs — are treated the same way. For example, "run of the mill" and "run-of-the-mill" are both treated as a single phrase in a search.

+ Put a plus sign (+) in front of a word that must appear in any document AltaVista finds for you.

+ Put a minus sign or hyphen (–) in front of a word that should *not* appear in any document AltaVista finds for you. This technique is extremely handy when you get flooded with responses you did not expect.

+ Make sure that you put a space before the + or – and no space between it and the word.

♦ AltaVista treats as a word any string of letters or numbers separated by a space or punctuation. For example, *USA* and *Year2000* are single words, *Year-2000* is a two-word phrase, and *U.S.A.* is a three-word phrase.

♦ AltaVista does not index punctuation.

♦ Don't direct your simple search with words such as AND, OR, and NOT or parentheses. AltaVista has an advanced search mode in which you *can* use these commands.

♦ Use the asterisk (*) wildcard character to search for variant spellings. For example, *Dumm** matches *Dummy, Dummy's,* and *Dummies.* AltaVista requires at least four characters before the *.

♦ If you don't like the answers you get, check your spelling and remove unnecessary capitalization; then try to express your search in different words.

Examples of search-word syntax are

```
repair "fax machine" +Chicago
"word processor" -Windows -DOS
job Mass* internet writer
```

Search strategies

♦ Start with the most naive search you can think of. If you want to rent a car in Madrid, for example, enter **Madrid car rental**.

♦ If you don't find what you want on the first page or two of search results, refine your search rather than look at more pages of results.

♦ Be ingenious in thinking up search words. Think of the search box as a sight with crosshairs. Try to find groups of words that slice the problem in two different directions.

♦ Describe narrowly what you want. Search for `Boston Red Sox` rather than `baseball teams`.

♦ Keep trying! You often have to do several searches to find what you want. Persistence pays.

♦ If you get many similar, irrelevant responses, find a word they all have in common and use the minus sign (–) feature. When you're looking for computers, for example, you search for `powerful processor`. If you get a dozen Cuisinart sites, change your request to `powerful processor -food`.

♦ Have fun. To sharpen your skills, practice looking up any crazy thing that interests you. Search for your name, company, school, or town!

✦ MetaSpy, from MetaCrawler, shows you ten recent searches other users have requested. It's entertaining and a fine source of search ideas, at `www.metaspy.com`.

✦ Bookmark pages you find interesting.

✦ If you find something you really need, save the page on your hard disk. The page may not be on the Web tomorrow.

✦ Never promise your boss that you will find something unless you've already found it and saved it away.

Excellent Surfing Ideas

✦ Look for someone you know. More and more people are mentioned at some site, somewhere. Search for the person's full name, and try the online telephone directories mentioned later in this part, in "Telephone Directories."

✦ Look up your illness. When you get diagnosed with something, look it up on the Internet. Look for the disease by name in a search engine or Web directory. Most diseases have at least one home page plus newsgroups and mailing lists (*see also* Parts IV and V).

✦ Visit a prospective employer's site before your interview. Search for the company's or organization's name.

✦ Get the form you need. More and more government agencies and private organizations have their forms available online. Get U.S. passport forms, for example, at `www.state.gov` and U.S. tax forms at `www.irs.ustreas.gov`.

✦ Find the book you want before you go to the library. Many libraries have their catalogs online, so you can even check whether the book you want is checked out.

✦ Do your shopping from home. Many major catalog companies have online shopping, and more and more storefront sites are opening up. (*See also* "Shopping Online from A to Z," later in this part.)

Free, Free, Free!

Quite a few companies think that the way to get rich on the Internet is to give stuff away. We don't know how long these free deals can last, although you may as well take advantage while they do.

We discuss free Internet access in Part II and free e-mail in Part III.

Here are some more free services:

+ **Free Fax:** eFax (`www.efax.com`) lets you receive fax messages over the Internet.

+ **Free phone service:** Call anywhere in the United States for as long as two minutes at `www.mytalk.com` — you can also check your e-mail by phone at this site. eFax also provides e-mail-by-phone.

+ **Free disk space:** I-drive (`www.idrive.com`) offers 25MB of free, online disk space, letting you access your files from any Web browser in the world. Freedrive (`www.freedrive.com`) gives you 20MB. You can also share files with friends, making these services a good alternative to e-mail attachments.

Information Sources

A great deal of geographical and other specialized information is on the Net.

The CIA's World Factbook

`www.cia.gov/cia/publications/factbook`

The almanac of the Internet, *The World Factbook* has detailed information about every country in the world, along with digital references, maps, and appendixes on international organizations.

Encyclopædia Britannica

The complete Encyclopedia Britannica is now available for free online, at `www.britannica.com`. The site also offers an index of carefully selected best-of-the-Web sites.

Libraries

Many libraries now have their card catalogs online. One of the best is the U.S. Library of Congress, at `www.loc.gov`, the world's largest library. In addition to having its card catalog online, the Library of Congress has pointers to a wide variety of Internet resources, both within and outside the United States government.

Some sites are devoted to making traditional books available online. Copyright laws restrict this service, for the most part, to older books and materials. One such site is the Online Book Initiative, at `obi.std.com`, which has gigabytes of classic texts available.

Maps

A number of sites provide maps, including detailed street maps, of the entire United States and many other countries:

- ✦ **Xerox PARC Map Server:** pubweb.parc.xerox.com/map

- ✦ **Official U.S. Gazetteer:** www.census.gov/cgibin/gazetteer (lets you find any geographic location in the United States)

- ✦ **Vicinity Corp. MapBlast:** www.mapblast.com

- ✦ **MapQuest:** www.mapquest.com

Microsoft's Terraserver (terraserver.microsoft.com) offers for free a vast collection of satellite and aerial photographs covering much of the Earth's surface.

Regional information providers

Directories such as Yahoo (*see also* "Directories, Search Engines, and Portals," earlier in this part) have sections devoted to local information. Many newspapers have their own Web sites with information about their service areas.

Most states and many cities in the United States have extensive Web sites. You can guess the URL for almost any city or state by using these templates:

- ✦ **For cities:** www.ci.cityname.XX.us

- ✦ **For states:** www.state.XX.us

XX is the two-letter state postal code; ma for Massachusetts, for example.

Satellites

Heavens Above (www.heavens-above.com/) alerts you to satellite passes visible from your location.

Statistics and other data

The U.S. Census Bureau (www.census.gov) has a wealth of data about the United States.

The United Nations offers a world data bank, including text of treaties, at www.un.org/databases.

World time

tycho.usno.navy.mil

If you need to know what time it is anywhere in the world, visit the Time Service department of the U.S. Naval Observatory, the United States government's official source of time.

Magazines and Literature

Most major magazines now have Web sites. Most use their name as their Web address; www.goodhousekeeping.com, for example. A wide range of *ezines* — magazines published online — is also available. A search for ezine and a topic often turns up something.

A thriving community of creative writers relishes the ability to reach an audience on the Internet without interminable cycles of submissions and rejections. You can check out their work or put up your own. Here are a few active sites:

+ **The Blue Moon Review:** www.thebluemoon.com

+ **A Small Garlic Press:** www.enteract.com/~asgp

+ **AfterDinner:** www.afterdinner.com

+ **The Zuzu's Petals Literary Resource:** www.zuzu.com

Music Online

A revolutionary technology named *MP3* is turning the recording industry upside down. Originally designed as the soundtrack for MPEG digital movies, MP3 lets anyone exchange musical recordings over the Internet. You need playback software, such as WinAMP (www.winamp.com) or SoundApp for the Mac, available at www.tucows.com. MP3 quality is good, but not quite as good as CDs.

You can buy small portable players, such as the Rio, www.rioport.com, which store hours of MP3 files downloaded from your computer. Many artists use MP3 and the Internet to distribute sample album cuts. Some Internet portals, such as Lycos (www.lycos.com), have separate sections devoted to MP3.

Anyone with a computer and a sound card can make MP3 files. Special programs called *rippers* are available that transfer cuts from your favorite CD to an MP3 file, although distributing ripped files may violate copyright laws. New CDs will soon contain sub-audible codes, called *digital watermarks*, to identify copyrighted material.

Microsoft is pushing a competing format named Windows Media Audio, or *WMA*. The recording industry has a new standard named *SDMI*, Secure Digital Music Initiative, that prevents unauthorized copying and allows music to be sold on the Internet. Portable players will soon be available that play both SMDI and MP3 files and enforce watermarking.

You can get more information about MPEG, including search engines for MPEG files, from MP3.com (www.mp3.com), PureMP3 (www.puremp3.org), and MP3now (www.mp3now.com).

Newspapers

Quite a few newspapers have built elaborate Web pages that include today's stories, archives of past stories, ads, and material created just for the Web. Some require you to register, and some even charge a subscription fee. Here are a few of the best:

✦ *The New York Times:* www.nytimes.com

✦ *The Wall Street Journal:* www.wsj.com (fee)

✦ *San Jose Mercury News:* www.sjmercury.com

✦ *The Boston Globe:* www.boston.com

Electronic newspapers on the Web can give you a customized news report. When you register, you select the topics you're interested in. The newspapers give you a page with hyperlink headlines about those topics every time you visit. Newspaper sites include

✦ **Cable News Network:** www.cnn.com

✦ **MSNBC,** a joint venture of Microsoft and the NBC television network in the United States: www.msnbc.com

✦ **My Yahoo!:** my.yahoo.com

EntryPoint, at www.entrypoint.com, offers a service that places on your screen a bar filled with breaking news, a personalized stock ticker, weather for cities you select, and more, along with lots of ads.

Infobeat, at www.infobeat.com, lets you sign up to get a daily news digest by e-mail, with links to longer stories on the Web. We love it!

Selling Online

Online auctions, eBay in particular, are revolutionizing Internet commerce. Anyone can list an item for sale, and a variety of auctions modes are supported. *Remember:* Let the buyer beware!

✦ **eBay:** www.ebay.com

✦ **Yahoo Auctions:** auctions.yahoo.com

eBay displays a feedback rating in parentheses next to each user ID. The rating is a numerical summary of all the feedback comments others have left about this user. If you click the number, you can read what others have said about that particular user.

If you have questions about the item in an auction listing, e-mail the seller.

When you're selling, describe your item as fully as possible. Try to anticipate questions people may ask. Tell how you want to be paid and who pays for shipping. Include a photo if at all possible.

Sellers can select several special types of auctions on eBay and other auction sites:

+ **Reserve Price Auctions:** Bidders know that sellers set a reserve price, although they don't know how much it is. To win the auction, a bidder must bid at least the reserve price.

+ **Private Auctions:** Bidders' e-mail addresses don't show up on the item or bidding-history screens. Only the seller knows who bought the item.

+ **Dutch Auctions:** Sellers list a minimum price and the number of items for sale. Bidders specify both a price and the quantity they want to buy, and all winning bidders pay the same price, which is the lowest successful bid. Higher bidders get the quantities they've asked for if there aren't enough to go around.

+ **Restricted-Access Auctions:** This category is for adult-only merchandise, and eBay requires bidders to have a verified credit card on file.

Next time you clean out your attic, list your junk on an Internet auction site. It may be someone else's treasure.

Shareware and Freeware Software

Downloading software used to be an ordeal. Now you can visit one of several software libraries on the Web, search for the software you want by name or function, read a review, and download the software with a click of your mouse. All the transmission and unpacking steps are done automatically by your browser if you have the necessary helper applications. (***See also*** the section in Part VI about plug-ins, helper programs, and ActiveX controls.)

This section describes some popular sites.

c|net Shareware.com

www.shareware.com

Shareware.com doesn't store software but rather helps you find sites that do, with a Virtual Software Library search engine. The site lets you search for, browse, and download shareware, freeware, commercial software, demos, fixes, patches, and upgrades from popular software archives and computer vendor sites all over the world. Shareware.com indexes Windows 98, Windows 95, Windows 3.*x*, Windows NT, Macintosh, OS/2, UNIX, Atari, Amiga, and Novell Netware software.

The Ultimate Collection of Winsock Software (TUCOWS)

www.tucows.com

Don't be misled by the name. TUCOWS now has a great collection of shareware for both Windows and Macintosh computers, if you can stand the cow puns. Because TUCOWS maintains its own copies of the programs at dozens of *mirror* (duplicate) sites, getting through and starting downloading is usually easy.

The Info-Mac Archive

ftp://ftp.amug.org/pub/info-machyperarchive.lcs.mit.edu/HyperArchive/HyperArchive.html

This site claims to have the largest collection of software for the Macintosh on the Internet. Info-Mac is maintained by volunteers who want to give something to the Macintosh community.

Shopping Online from A to Z

Most people have never purchased anything, let alone sold anything, over the Internet. Yet, in a few years, Internet commerce will become as commonplace as mail-order catalogs and classified ads. This section presents a sampling of what you can find on the Internet; the list is intended to be inspirational rather than comprehensive. To find what you're looking for, try the search engines described earlier in this part or visit

www.yahoo.com/Business_and_Economy/Companies/Shopping_Centers/Online_Shopping

(Rather than type that entire URL, just start out at www.yahoo.com and choose Business and Economy, Companies, Shopping Centers, and then Online Shopping.) The regional Usenet hierarchies usually have a forsale group. For example, la.forsale covers Los Angeles. (*See also* Part IV to find out how to read Usenet newsgroups.)

Do you have junk in your house you don't need but can't bear to throw out? A message to a relevant Usenet `forsale` group can find someone who would be happy to cart it away.

Airlines

Most airlines now have Web pages, and many enable you to make reservations online. Some even offer last-minute specials to try to fill their flights. Some airline sites are better than others, and using an airlines' tollfree number is often easier. John maintains an extensive collection of airline links, at `www.iecc.com/airline`.

Also visit the Usenet group `rec.travel.air`, or try a Deja.com search for your destination. (***See also*** "Deja.com and Usenet Indexers," in Part IV.)

Books

Bookselling has been the most successful online business so far, we hear (other than porn, anyway):

+ **Amazon.com** (`www.amazon.com`) is the poster girl for the Internet's commercial potential. A well-implemented Web site for buying books became the world's largest bookstore.

+ **Barnes and Noble** (`www.bn.com`) — the world's largest online bookseller is challenged by the world's largest bookseller online.

+ **Borders.com** (`www.borders.com`) is the third of the big three online bookstores. Like Amazon and B&N, it has branched out into videos and music, too.

+ **Schoenhof's Foreign Books** (`www.schoenhofs.com`) carries books in languages other than English.

Condoms

The embarrassment of going through the checkout line with a box of condoms can be a thing of the past. Condom Country (`www.condom.com`) ships them in a plain brown box, and its selection is much better.

Dolls and other collectibles

The Web is revolutionizing the market for collectibles with active newsgroups targeted to the narrowest of interests, including `rec.collecting.dolls` and two dozen different newsgroups in the `rec.collecting`, `rec.antiques`, and `alt.collecting` hierarchies.

Electronic auction sites are another great place for collectibles fans. (***See also*** "Selling Online," earlier in this part.)

Education

Almost every school and college has an extensive Web site. You can find a complete list at www.yahoo.com/education.

Many college Web sites have areas for student home pages. You can contact students whose interests match yours and find out what the school is really like.

Flowers

Make amends for all that time you're spending online these days:

✦ **1-800-FLOWERS:** www.1800flowers.com

✦ **FlowerLink:** www.flowerlink.com

Groceries

Why fight with a grocery cart?

✦ **Peapod Home Grocery Delivery:** www.peapod.com

✦ **Homeruns:** www.homeruns.com

Houses

Yahoo maintains an extensive list of real estate resources, including classified ads, at:

realestate.classifieds.yahoo.com/resources/
    realestate.html

Internet service providers

✦ **The List:** thelist.internet.com

✦ **The Directory:** www.thedirectory.org

Jobs

More and more people are finding their jobs or hiring people on the Net. Yahoo has a well-organized list of employment resources, at www.yahoo.com/Business/Employment.

The Usenet hierarchy is another great source: misc.jobs has more than a dozen groups. Regional groups exist too; for example, ne.jobs covers the northeast United States.

Love

Find that special someone, but be careful! Try Match, at www.match.com.

Macintoshes

Apple Computer is now selling computers online at www.apple. com. If you're looking for Mcintosh apples, not Apple Macintoshes, try www.redapplefarm.com. It ships a gift box of the yummy fruit almost anywhere.

Overcoats and boots

+ **L.L. Bean:** www.llbean.com
+ **Lands' End:** www.landsend.com

Postage

Stamps.com (stamps.com) and e-stamp (e-stamp.com) let you print postage stamps as you print envelopes or labels on your own laser or inkjet printer. Fees start at $2 per month plus postage.

Quesadillas

Microsoft Sidewalk (www.sidewalk.com) and CitySearch (www.citysearch.com) list restaurants by cuisine in the areas they serve.

Stocks and bonds

Online trading can slash transaction costs for small investors, although the investment risk remains. Here are a few popular online brokers:

+ **Charles Schwab Online:** www.schwab.com
+ **Datek Online Broker:** www.datek.com
+ **E*Trade:** www.etrade.com
+ **Fidelity Investments:** www.fidelity.com
+ **T. Rowe Price:** www.troweprice.com

Tapes and CDs

+ **CDNOW:** www.cdnow.com
+ **Reel.com:** www.reel.com
+ **Great Tapes for Kids:** Run by our own Margy and her family, at www.greattapes.com

Used and new cars

✦ **AutoByTel:** To compare prices of new and used cars, see autobytel.com. It works with local dealers to quote you a price.

✦ **Carfax:** You can check publicly available records to learn that cream puff's true history, at www.carfax.com.

Vitamins

To your health! Visit www.vitaminshoppe.com.

Web page design

If you want that professional look, browse oodles of listings by starting at Yahoo (www.yahoo.com) and choosing Business and Economy, Companies, Internet Services, Web Services, and then Designers.

Xylophones

Look up your favorite musical instrument on a search engine or on Deja.com. We found these two:

✦ **Musser Xylophones:** www.ludwig-drums.com/xylo.htm

✦ **Neptune's Joinery:**
www.coffsharbour.com/Neptunes/xylo.html

Yiddish

Books and instruction in the *mama loshen:*

✦ **The National Yiddish Book Center:** www.yiddishbookcenter.org

✦ **The Yiddish Voice:** www.yv.org

Zygotes

The American Surrogacy Center (www.surrogacy.com) says that it's the most complete source of surrogacy and egg donation information on the Web.

"Should I Give Out My Credit Card Number over the Internet?"

Two different views on this practice prevail.

One camp says that because so many other ways are available for crooks to steal credit card numbers, why worry about sending yours over the Net? Crooks can fish a discarded paper receipt from a Dumpster much more easily than they can intercept messages on the Net. In the United States, a credit card holder's liability in cases of fraud is limited to $50 per card. (***Warning:*** *Debit* cards have a higher limit.)

The other camp counters that computer use enables fraud to occur on a much more massive scale than have past methods. The best technology available, therefore, should be used to make cyberspace as safe as possible, and everyone should insist on secure links before using the Internet for credit card and other financial transactions.

If you're going to give out your credit card number online, we strongly recommend that you get a version of your favorite browser with U.S. or 128-bit security. Also, before entering your credit card number, make sure that the closed-lock icon, indicating a secure connection, appears in the lower-left corner of your browser window. (***See also*** "Internet Explorer and Netscape Communicator," in Part IX.)

Telephone Directories

Several Web sites offer complete "white pages" coverage: listings of home phone numbers for North America and many other countries. Most also offer e-mail addresses, selected businesses, and yellow pages listings. These Web sites are a great way to locate long-lost friends. (***See also*** the section in Part III about finding e-mail addresses.)

✦ **CBS Switchboard:** `www.switchboard.com`

✦ **WhoWhere from Lycos:** `whowhere.com`

✦ **Yahoo People Search:** `people.yahoo.com`

Uncompressing and Decoding Retrieved Files

After you download a file, your Web browser can often display the information in the file. Because some files require a special plug-in or helper application (***see also*** Part VI), you may have to do some more work before you can use the file:

✦ Files on anonymous FTP systems are usually stored in compressed format. Compressed files are in one of several special formats that squeeze the file so that it takes up less space in memory and takes less time to transmit over the Net.

✦ Often, files are *archived* too, which means that a group of files is strung together as one file.

✦ Some files are pictures or images that require particular programs to display them.

Remember: The filename *extension* (the part after the dot) tells you how the file is coded and (more important) which program to use to decode it.

You can download compression and uncompression programs from the Web. (*See also* "Shareware and Freeware Software," earlier in this part.)

Download WinZip or ZipMagic (for Windows machines) or StuffIt Expander and DropStuff with Expander Enhancer (for Macintoshes) so that you can handle most compressed and archived formats. (*See also* the section in Part VI about plug-ins, helper programs, and ActiveX controls.)

Be sure to check downloaded files for viruses. (*See also* "Viruses," later in this part.)

The following table lists the main categories of files found on the Web:

File Type	Description
Archived	Many files combined into one (most archived files are also compressed)
Compressed	A coded form that saves space, with many variants
Images	Digitized pictures in GIF, JPEG, or other graphics formats
Sound	Digitized sounds in MP3, WAV, AIFF, or other audio formats
Video	Digitized pictures in MPEG, QuickTime, or other video formats
Text	Plain text that can be printed, displayed, and edited with the usual printing and text-editing programs
Encoded	Special formats (like MIME or uuencoding) that disguise a nontext file as text so that it can be e-mailed

The most common extensions for files found on the Web are described in the following sections.

.gif

CompuServe GIF (Graphics Interchange Format) is a popular image format. Graphical browsers, such as Internet Explorer and Netscape Navigator, display GIF files directly, without help from a plug-in.

.gz and .z

Files with the extensions .gz and .z (lowercase) are created by the gzip program, from the Free Software Foundation GNU project. They're uncompressed by GNU gunzip, Expander Enhancer, and WinZip. GNU gunzip can uncompress many other compressed formats too.

WinZip, gzip, and gunzip are available from Web shareware sites.

.hqx

The .hqx extension is for files in the Macintosh BinHex format. StuffIt Expander (for Windows) and StuffIt Expander and DropStuff with Expander Enhancer (for the Macintosh) handle this format. You can download them from Web shareware sites.

.jpeg and .jpg

JPEG (Joint Photographic Experts Group) is a popular compressed-image format. Most browsers display JPEG files directly, without help from a plug-in. JPEG images often have the extensions .jpeg, .jpg, or .jif.

.mp3

MPEG Level 3 is widely used to exchange musical recordings over the Internet. (*See also* "Music Online," earlier in this part.")

.mpeg and .mpg

MPEG (Motion Picture Experts Group) is a popular compressed-video format. MPEG images often have the extension .mpeg or .mpg.

.sit

This one is a Macintosh StuffIt archive. StuffIt Expander handles this format. You can download it from Web shareware sites.

.tar

Files with the extension .tar are the products of tar (Tape ARchive), a UNIX archiving program. To unpack a tar file on a UNIX system, type **tar xvf blurfle.tar**.

Tar files are also commonly compressed and have names such as blurfle.tar.Z. Uncompress them, and then unpack. On some systems, these files are called TAZ files. WinZip and StuffIt Expander Enhancer can unscramble them.

.Z

Files with the extension .Z (uppercase) are compressed files created by the UNIX compress program. They're decoded with the UNIX uncompress program, StuffIt Expander Enhancer, or WinZip.

.zip

Files with the extension .zip are compressed archives created by the shareware program PKZIP or free ZIP utilities, and they can be unpacked with the shareware program PKUNZIP, the free program UNZIP, StuffIt Expander with Expander Enhancer, or WinZip. ZipMagic (www.mijenix.com) makes ZIP files look like folders on Windows computers — very convenient.

These programs are available from most Web shareware sites. WinZip is also available at www.winzip.com.

Viruses

Viruses are small, mischievous computer programs that can spread from computer to computer when files are shared. Downloading an infected program and running it on your computer is one way your computer can become infected.

If you don't have an up-to-date virus program on your computer, try McAfee VirusScan (www.mcafee.com/centers/anti-virus) or Norton AntiVirus (www.symantec.com/nav).

Here are some tips for protecting your computer without becoming paranoid:

✦ Because viruses can damage files, the most important step you can take to protect yourself is to back up your hard disk regularly.

✦ Do not discard or reuse old backup media until you have checked your entire hard disk for viruses.

✦ Viruses can infect word-processing files created by Microsoft Word and spreadsheet files created by Microsoft Excel. For more information about this vexing problem, see the Microsoft Support page support.microsoft.com/support and request article number Q163932 from the Microsoft Knowledge Base (KB): "Word 97: Frequently Asked Questions About Word Macro Viruses."

✦ Virus-checking programs are available for most personal computers. You can use them to check individual files, directories, or your entire hard disk.

✦ Most virus-checking programs require that any file be decompressed first before being checked.

✦ Always virus-check any software you do not receive directly from the manufacturer or commercial distributor. Be particularly careful about programs and Word files you download from the Internet or receive as an e-mail attachment or from friends and acquaintances via floppy disk.

✦ Most large shareware-archive sites check the programs they receive for computer viruses. Because you can never be too careful, virus-checking *any* software before using it is a good idea.

✦ Virus-check your entire hard disk, and then back it up at least once a month.

A regular hoax that circulates on the Internet involves some e-mail you're not supposed to open, lest your computer become infected with a virus. Although e-mail messages themselves cannot contain viruses, files attached to e-mail messages *can* be infected. Don't open files attached to e-mail you receive from strangers. Even files you receive from friends can be infected — if you weren't expecting a file from that person, write back first to make sure that the message wasn't sent by a virus!

Part VIII

Live Online Communication

The Internet lets you communicate with people in a more immediate way than sending electronic mail and waiting hours or days for a reply. You can type something, press Enter, and get a reply within seconds — a process called *instant messaging* or *chatting*. You can also use the Internet for voice and even video communication. In this part, we tell you about the most popular forms of online communication and how to get the most from them.

In this part . . .

- ✔ Before you start chatting
- ✔ Chatting on America Online
- ✔ Chatting on ICQ
- ✔ Chatting on IRC
- ✔ Chatting on the Web
- ✔ Playing in the MUDs
- ✔ Using Internet telephone and video phones

Chatting Online

Online chat lets you communicate with people live, just as you would do on the telephone — except that you type what you want to say and read the other person's reply on your computer screen. An entire Internet subculture has grown up around chat.

If you have never had an online chat, you may find the idea cold and uninviting. You can, in fact, make real emotional contact with another person, even a stranger, through online chat; it takes getting used to, however. Here are some things you need to know about chat:

+ In chat, a window shows the ongoing conversation. You type in a separate box what you want to send to the individual or group. When you press Enter or click the Send button, your message appears in the conversation window, along with any responses.

+ Chat differs from e-mail in that you don't have to address each message and wait for a reply. Though sometimes a small lag occurs in chatting, communication is nearly instantaneous — even across the globe.

+ You're usually limited to a sentence or two in each exchange. Instant messages, described later in this part, allow longer expressions.

+ You can select a group or an individual to chat with, or someone can ask to initiate a private chat with you. Many chat venues exist on the Net, including IRC (Internet Relay Chat), AOL chat rooms (for AOL users only), Web-based chat, and instant messaging systems like ICQ and AIM (AOL Instant Messenger).

+ Because tens of thousands of people are chatting at any instant of the day or night, the discussions are divided into groups. Different terms exist for chat groups. AOL and ICQ calls them *rooms.* IRC (Internet Relay Chat) calls them *channels.*

+ The chat facilities of the value-added service providers are accessible to only that service's members. Only AOL members can use the AOL chat rooms, for example. You cannot get to the AOL chat rooms from ICQ or IRC.

+ People in chat groups can be unruly and even vicious. The online service providers' chat groups usually are tamer because the service provides some supervision.

+ You may select a special name — a *screen name, handle,* or *nickname* — to use when you're chatting. This name can and often does differ from your login name or e-mail address.

Although your special chat name gives you some privacy online, someone could possibly find out your real identity, particularly if your online service or ISP cooperates. Don't go wild out there.

Conversations: They can be hard to follow

Get used to following a group conversation if you want to make any sense of chats. Here's a sample of what you may see (screen names and identifying content have been changed):

```
BrtG221: hey Zeb!
Zebra795: Hello
ABE904: Where is everyone from......I am from
        Virginia
Zebra795: Hi Brt!
HAPY F: how should I know
Zebra795: Hi ABE
HAPY F: <--Virginia
ABE904: Hi Zebra!!!
BrtG221: so StC... what
Zebra795: <--was from Virginia!
ABE904: Hi HAPY ! Didn't see ya
BrtG221: is going on in FL?
HAPY F: HI ABE
Zebra795: Hap's been on all night!
Storm17: Brt...what?...i miss our heart to hearts
HAPY F: on and off
ABE904: Zeb, and wish you were back here!
DDouble6190: im 26 but i like older women
Zebra795: I was over July Fourth!!
Janet5301: Sorry...DD...call me in 10 yrs...
BrtG221: really DD?... where do you live?
BrtG221: lol.. so talk to me Storm..
ABE904: Gee, you didn't call, didn't write....
```

Here are a few tips for getting started:

✦ When you enter a chat group, a conversation is usually already in progress. You cannot see what went on before you entered.

✦ Wait a minute or two for a page full of exchanges to appear onscreen so that you can understand some of their context before you start reading.

✦ Start by following the comments from a single screen name. Then follow the people whom that person mentions or who reply to that person. Ignore everything else because the other messages are probably replies to messages that went by before you came in.

✦ After you can follow one thread, try picking up another. It takes practice to get the hang of it.

+ Some services, such as AOL, let you highlight the messages from one or more screen names. This capability can make things easier to follow.

+ You can also indicate screen names to ignore. Messages from these chatters no longer appear onscreen, though other members' replies to them do appear.

+ Scroll up to see older messages if you have to, and remember that after you have scrolled up, new messages don't appear until you scroll back down.

+ Many of the messages are greetings to familiar names as they join or leave the chat group.

+ A few regulars often dominate the conversation.

+ The real action often takes place in private, one-on-one side discussions, which you cannot see.

Etiquette for chatting

Chatting etiquette isn't much different from e-mail (**see also** "Electronic etiquette," in Part III), and common sense is your best online guide. Here are some additional chat behavior tips:

+ The first rule of chat is that a real person with real feelings is at the other end of the computer chat connection. Hurting him or her is not okay.

+ The second rule is that because you really have no idea who that other person is, being cautious is okay. **See also** the following section.

+ Read messages for a while to figure out what is happening before sending a message to a chat group.

+ Keep your comments short and to the point.

+ Avoid insults and foul language.

+ Many systems let you create a profile about yourself, which other members can access. Having a profile is polite. You don't have to tell everything about yourself in your profile, although what you do say should be truthful.

+ If you want to talk to someone in private, send a message saying Hi, who you are, and what you want.

+ More people are out there whom you don't want to meet than people whom you do, although quite a few potential friends are chatting too. If the rudeness and banality of chat turn you off at first, try other groups.

For more information about the history and art of meeting pι
online, see Philippe Le Roux's article, "Virtual Intimacy — Talε
from Minitel and More," at `net.gurus.com/leroux.phtml`.

Safe chatting

Here are some guidelines for conducting safe and healthy chats:

+ Many people in chat groups are totally dishonest about who
  they are. They lie about their occupation, age, locality, and,
  yes, even gender. Some just think that they're being cute, and
  others are exploring their own fantasies; a few are really sick.

+ Be careful about giving out information that enables someone
  to find you personally, including phone numbers, mailing
  address, and schools your kids attend.

+ AT&T has a service that lets you talk to someone you meet
  in a chat room *without* exchanging phone numbers. Visit
  `chatntalk.att.com` for details.

+ Pick a screen name or handle that's different from your login
  name; otherwise, you will receive a great deal of unwanted junk
  e-mail.

+ Never give out your password to anyone, even if she says that
  she works for your service provider, the phone company, the
  FBI, the CIA, or Dummies Press. Never!

+ If your chat service offers profiles and a person without a profile wants to chat with you, be extra cautious.

+ If your children use chat, realize that others may try to meet
  them. Before your kids log on, spend some quality time with
  them, going over the guidelines in "Kids, Porn, and the Web," in
  Part VI.

+ Don't hesitate to report anyone who you believe is behaving
  inappropriately on a value-added service's chat group. On AOL,
  go to keyword **Notify AOL**. On CompuServe, go to the keyword
  feedback.

If you choose to meet an online friend in person, use at least the
same caution you would use in meeting someone through a newspaper ad:

+ Don't arrange a meeting until you have talked to that person a
  number of times over the course of days or weeks.

+ Have a few phone conversations first.

+ Meet in a public place.

+ Bring a friend along, if possible. If not, at least let someone else know what you're doing and agree to call that person at a specified time, (a half-hour, for example) after the meeting time.

+ If you travel a long distance to meet someone, stay in a hotel, not at that person's home.

A description of other important precautions is beyond the scope of this book. See *Sex For Dummies,* by Dr. Ruth Westheimer (IDG Books Worldwide, Inc.), for more information.

Smileys, abbreviations, and emoticons

Chat abbreviations are similar to those used in news and e-mail (*see also* "Abbreviations and Acronyms" and "Smileys and Emoticons," in Part III), although some are unique to the real-time nature of chat. Here's a list of abbreviations and emoticons common on AOL and other chat services:

AFK	Away From Keyboard
A/S/L	Age/Sex/Location (response may be 35/f/LA)
BAK	Back At Keyboard
BRB	Be Right Back
BTW	By The Way
FTF	Face To Face
GMTA	Great Minds Think Alike
IC	In Character (playing a role)
ICQ	A chat service described later in this part
IM	Instant Message
IMHO	In My Humble Opinion
IRC	Internet Relay Chat, a chat service described later in this part
LTNS	Long Time No See
LOL	Laughing Out Loud
M4M	Men seeking other men
OOC	Out Of Character (stepping out of a role)
RL	Real Life (opposite of RP)
ROTFL	Rolling On The Floor Laughing
RP	Role Play (acting a character in a fantasy)
TOS	Terms of Service (the AOL member contract)
TTFN	Ta-Ta For Now!

WB	Welcome Back
WTG	Way To Go!
:) or : -)	Smile
: D	Smile/laughing/big grin
**	Kisses
;)	Wink
{ }	Hug
: (or : - (	Frown
: ' (	Crying
0 :)	Angel
} : >	Devil
: X	My lips are sealed
: P	Sticking out tongue
(_|_)	Moon

Weeding out disruptive chatters

Some people take advantage of the anonymity chat provides and get quite rude. You have four good options and one bad option when this situation happens.

Here are some good options:

✦ **Go to another chat room.** Some rooms are just nasty. You don't have to hang around.

✦ **Pay no attention to the troublemaker.** Just converse with the other folks.

✦ **Make the person's comments disappear from your screen.** On AOL, double-click the jerk's screen name on the room list and then click the Ignore box. On CompuServe, you can create a Prohibited Users list; on the Chat Desktop, choose Chat⇨ Modify Prohibited List from the menu to create a list of people whose comments you want to ignore.

✦ **Complain to the individual's service provider.** This option is most effective on the value-added services. *See also* "Filing a complaint," later in this part.

The bad option is responding in kind, which just gives the offender the attention he (usually he) wants and may get *you* kicked off your service.

Chatting on America Online (AOL)

Chat lets AOL users meet and have a conversation with other AOL users. People Connection is one of the most popular features AOL provides. The quality of AOL chat is a major reason that it's the largest value-added service provider. This section describes chatting by using America Online 5.0 software.

Beginning to chat

To start chatting, click the Chat icon in the Welcome window or click the People icon on the toolbar and choose People Connection from the menu that appears; or go to keyword **chat**. You see the People Connection window; click the Chat Now button to enter a lobby room (the window is labeled Town Square plus the number of the lobby). An online conversation appears in the large text window. A smaller window, the People here list, lists all the people in the room.

If you double-click a screen name from the People here list, a window pops up and gives you three options:

+ **Ignore Member:** Check this box to no longer see messages from this member.

+ **Send Message:** Click here to send this member an Instant Message.

+ **Get Profile:** Click here to see this member's profile, if it exists.

You may find what you want in the lobby room, but we doubt it. To see a list of other rooms you can visit, click the Find a Chat icon to see the Find a Chat window. The list on the left shows categories of rooms; click one and click the View Chats button. The chat rooms in that category appear on the list on the right. Click the room you want to visit and click Go Chat. AOL takes you to that room, maybe.

AOL limits the number of members that can be in any one room, usually to about 23 people. Some rooms are extremely popular, and AOL automatically creates additional copies of that type of room as earlier rooms of that type fill up.

Rooms with a view

The conversation in most rooms is pretty thin. Finding one you like takes some effort. Poke around. Look for a room with a narrow charter — locality, hobbies, medical problems, age, or religion, for example — that matches your interests.

AOL groups rooms into categories. AOL People Connection creates standard rooms in each category, and members create additional ones:

+ **Lobby:** You're automatically in a lobby room when you go to the People Connection. Because many people never leave the lobby room, it's not uncommon to be in a room named Lobby 234 — which means that 233 other lobby rooms were created before this one.

+ **Town Square:** This area contains lobbies and other meeting rooms. The names of Town Square chat rooms vary, although they all feel about the same.

+ **Arts & Entertainment:** Rooms are organized around pop culture themes, with simulated bars, trivia quizzes, Trekkies, and other fun stuff.

+ **Friends:** Somewhat lower-key than the Romance groups, at least in theory.

+ **Life:** This area has a variety of lifestyles, from born-agains to gays to born-again gays.

+ **News, Sports, Finance:** Money, politics, and jocks are here.

+ **Places:** Organized by major metropolitan areas in the United States.

+ **Romance:** You see all the variations on boy meets girl, boy meets boy, girl meets girl — you name it.

+ **Special Interests:** Meet people interested in certain hobbies, pets, computers, or whatever.

+ **Country-specific rooms:** For example, Canada, eh!

+ **Member rooms:** You have to click the Created by AOL Members tab on the Find a Chat window to see these rooms. Anyone can create a member room by clicking the icon marked Start Your Own Chat. Many member rooms are locality-specific. A few are serious. Most are silly or kinky.

Not all AOL rooms appear on the Find a Chat screen. Some groups have their own chat areas that aren't listed here. You can sometimes find them by looking on the AOL Lifestyles channel. Or just try guessing the keyword.

Choosing a screen name

AOL uses your login name as your screen name unless you make up a special screen name. Many people use a separate screen name in chat to preserve their anonymity. To make a new screen name when you're online:

1. Click the My <u>A</u>OL button on the toolbar and choose Scree<u>n</u> Names from the menu that appears (or go to keyword **names**). You see the Create or Delete Screen Names window. (If you haven't done this step, you may want to double-click About Screen Names to get some background.)

2. Double-click Create a Screen Name.

3. Type a new screen name. (The one you want may be taken — all the good names are, in fact — so be creative.)

4. Click the Create A Screen Name button. AOL checks whether the name you typed is already used by someone else. If it is, you see a message to that effect; click OK and return to Step 3.

5. Fill out the rest of the information AOL requires for a new screen name, including the password.

AOL lets you have as many as seven screen names. The names can be used for other family members, for example. You have to create the new name on your main account. To get rid of a screen name you no longer plan to use, double-click Delete a Screen Name in Step 2 in this set of steps.

Filing a complaint

AOL has rules governing online behavior; you can review its Terms of Service (TOS) agreement by going to keyword **tos** (terms of service). If a situation gets really bad, you can report a violation on the Terms of Service window or go to keyword **Notify AOL**. Typing the keyword **guidepager** asks an AOL official to visit the chat room and set things straight.

Instant messages

You can "IM" anyone in a chat room. To start an IM session, double-click the person's name on a room list and click Send Message. You can also click the <u>P</u>eople icon on the toolbar and choose <u>I</u>nstant Message (or press Ctrl+I) and then type the member's screen name.

When someone sends you an IM, that person's message appears in a small window; if your computer has sound, you hear a distinctive chime. Respond by typing in the lower half of the window whatever you want to say. Then click Send. You can continue the conversation by typing in the lower window, clicking Send, and then reading the response in the upper window.

AOL now lets other people on the Internet exchange instant messages for free. This AOL Instant Messenger service (AIM) also supports the Buddy List feature, described in "Buddy Lists," later in this part.

Internet users can download the necessary software and register their screen names at www.aol.com. Instant Messenger also comes as part of Netscape Communicator. AOL users don't have to do anything to participate, although they can find out more by going to keyword **instant messenger**.

Private rooms

Private rooms let you chat with other members a little more conveniently than by using Instant Messages, and you can have more than two people in a private room.

Any AOL member can create a private room. To visit one, you have to determine the name of the room. Then click the Private Chat icon in the Town Square window, type that name, and click Go Chat.

To create your own room, start in the Find a Chat window, click Start Your Own Chat, and choose to start a private chat. For the name, type a name that's not in use. *Remember:* You cannot see a list of private room names — that's what makes them private!

Private rooms have a somewhat sleazy connotation. If you're invited into one, you may be approached to have *cybersex,* which is an exchange of intimate messages designed to arouse each other. Digital pillow talk may not be your cup of tea; if you give it a try, however, remember these guidelines:

✦ Some members lie about anything, especially gender.

✦ Occasionally, a member doesn't take no for an answer and may continue to pester you.

✦ It's not considered polite to send an Instant Message to someone who is in a private room.

✦ Respect the privacy of the other person or persons in the room.

✦ Remember that other people may not respect your privacy. Your conversation can be saved to a file and even shown to others.

Profiles

Your profile tells other members a little about you. Create your profile by clicking the My AOL icon on the toolbar and choosing My Member Profile from the menu that appears. When you see the Edit Your Online Profile window, fill out the form and click Update.

Look at another member's profile by double-clicking the person's screen name on the list of people in a room and clicking the Get Profile button. You can also click the People icon on the toolbar and choose Get AOL Member Profile from the menu that appears (or press Ctrl+G). Then type a screen name and click OK.

Buddy Lists

Buddy Lists save you the trouble of searching to see which of your chat friends are online at the moment. When a buddy logs on, AOL lets you know in the Buddy List window. (You can see the Buddy List window at any time by clicking the People icon on the toolbar and choosing View Buddy List from the menu that appears.) You can then find which chat room they're in by clicking the Locate icon or send them an Instant Message by clicking the IM icon.

You can make several Buddy Lists, each one for a different group of buddies. For example, you may have one for business associates and one for people who share your interest in vegetarian Indian cooking. To create a Buddy List:

1. Click the My AOL icon on the toolbar and choose Buddy List. You see your Buddy Lists window, with a list of the Buddy Lists you've already made, if any.

2. Click the Create button. You see the Create a Buddy List Group window.

3. Type a name for your new list in the Buddy List Group Name box.

4. Type in the Enter a Screen Name box the screen name of a friend you want on this list and then click Add Buddy. The screen name appears in the Buddies in Group box.

Repeat this step for each person you want on this list.

5. Click Save.

Your Buddy Lists window also lets you edit your Buddy Lists, search the AOL member directory, and set your Buddy List and Privacy preferences. Click Buddy List Preferences to control whether AOL shows you the Buddy List when you sign on. Click Privacy Preferences to control who may send you an Instant Message.

Making sounds

You can make other members' computers sound off by typing a message with the name of a special file between asterisks. For example, sending the message *goodbye* causes everyone in the chat room to hear the familiar AOL "good-bye" sound. Some versions of the AOL software require that you type {S (an open curly brace and an *S*) followed by a space and the filename. Try both — maybe one method will work for you.

These special .wav files are called *wave files,* or *sound files.* You can download many sound files from www.nwlaser.com/wavs (some

have adult content). You must put them in the same directory as
your AOL program.

Although chat sounds are fun occasionally, every now and then
someone in a room goes overboard and blasts out your speakers.
To turn off the sound feature, click the My <u>A</u>OL icon on the toolbar,
choose <u>P</u>references, click the Chat icon, and uncheck the Enable
chat room sounds box.

ICQ

ICQ, pronounced "I seek you," is a popular program that lets you
chat and exchange messages and files with other ICQ users.
Developed by an Israeli company, Mirabilis, and sold to AOL, ICQ
has more than 20,000,000 users.

Even though ICQ is now owned by AOL, ICQ doesn't allow you to
communicate with AOL chat or Instant Messages.

Getting ICQ

ICQ is available for Windows and Macintosh, and a Java version
is also available. You can download ICQ from www.icq.com or
www.tucows.com. A good alternative Macintosh version is available from www.gerryicq.com.

ICQ asks a number of personal questions for marketing purposes
when you first register. You don't have to answer the questions to
use ICQ. Parents should review the questions with their kids before
letting their kids sign up.

Making contact

Using ICQ is a little complicated at first, compared to e-mail:

+ You have to add a user to your contact list before you can send
  him a message.

+ Each ICQ user is assigned an identification number. Knowing a
  user's ID number helps when you're building your contact list.
  After that, you don't need to know the number.

+ ICQ lets you find another user by name, nickname, or e-mail
  address as well as by number.

+ You can chat with other ICQ users whenever you and they are
  connected to the Internet at the same time. You can send messages and files at any time.

+ When your ICQ friends are online, ICQ moves their names to
  the top of your contact list.

To add someone to your contact list:

1. Click the Add/Find Users button in the ICQ window.

You see the Add/Find Users window, which lists a number of different search methods.

2. Choose one of the search methods and fill in the information it requests.

3. Click Next. If the search finds more than one match, you're asked to click the user you want added to your list.

At the time you register, you can ask ICQ to notify you whenever someone wants to add you to her contact list. It's best to know who your contacts are.

Let's chat

To initiate a chat session with someone:

1. Right-click the person's name on your contact list. (Mac users, click the arrow icon to the right of the name.)

2. Choose ICQ Chat from the User menu.

3. Type in the text box a brief message that tells what you want to chat about.

4. Click the Chat button.

Your message is sent to the user you requested, who, we trust, will favor you with a reply.

If an ICQ user wants to chat with you, a flashing chat icon appears. Double-click the icon and choose Accept in the window that appears.

ICQ has chat rooms on a variety of topics, although they're not related to and not as good as the regular AOL chat rooms.

Take a message

To send a message to someone on your contact list:

1. Open the ICQ window and right-click the person's name. (Mac users, click the arrow icon to the right of the name.)

2. Click the message button in the send area of the User menu.

3. Type the message in the text box.

4. Click the Send button.

When an ICQ user wants to contact you, a flashing icon appears next to his name. Double-click this icon to see the message or start a chat session.

Filing a complaint

ICQ has an acceptable-use policy and frowns on various forms of abuse. However, given its huge user base and free service, don't expect a great deal of support. To inform ICQ of a serious problem, visit `www.mirabilis.com/contact2.html`.

Internet Relay Chat (IRC)

Internet Relay Chat (IRC) is the Internet's own chat service. IRC is available from most Internet Service Providers. You can even participate in IRC through most online services, though IRC is completely separate from the service's own chat services.

You need an *IRC client program* (or just *IRC program*), which is another Internet program, like your Web browser or e-mail program. Freeware and shareware IRC programs are available for you to download from the Net. Most UNIX systems come with an IRC program. Two of the best shareware IRC programs are

✦ mIRC, for Windows

✦ Ircle, for Macintosh

You can download these programs and get detailed information about installing them from `deckard.mc.duke.edu`. They're also available from TUCOWS (`www.tucows.com`). Windows 98 comes with Microsoft Chat. (You may have to install it from your Windows 98 CD-ROM.)

Check with your Internet provider for any additional information you may need in order to use IRC. If you have a direct link to the Internet, ask your system administrator whether the link supports IRC.

You use IRC in two main ways:

✦ *Channels:* Like an ongoing conference call with a bunch of people. After you join a channel, you can read what people are saying onscreen and then add your own comments just by typing them and pressing Enter.

✦ *Direct connection:* Like a private conversation.

Starting IRC

1. Connect to the Internet and run your IRC program.

2. Connect to an IRC server. (*See also* the following section to find out how.)

3. Join a channel. (*See also* "IRC channels," later in this section.)

You're ready to chat!

If you're on a value-added service, follow its instructions for connecting to the Internet. If you're using a UNIX shell Internet provider that offers IRC, type **ircii** or **irc** at the UNIX prompt.

Picking a server

To use IRC, you connect your IRC program to an *IRC server,* an Internet host computer that serves as a switchboard for IRC conversations. Although dozens of IRC servers are available, many are full most of the time and may refuse your connection. You may have to try several servers, or the same one dozens of times, before you can connect.

When you're choosing a server, pick one that's geographically close to you to minimize response lag. The Undernet servers are particularly popular.

To connect to a server:

✦ In mIRC, choose File⇨Setup or press Alt+E to display the mIRC Setup window and then click the IRC Servers tab. When you start mIRC, it gives this command for you automatically, so you see the mIRC Setup window right away. Double-click a server on the list to attempt to connect to it.

✦ In Ircle, choose File⇨Preferences⇨Startup. Select a server and then choose File⇨Save Preferences.

If at first you don't connect, try, try again.

Issuing IRC commands

You control what is happening during your chat session by typing IRC commands. All IRC commands start with the slash character (/). You can type IRC commands in upper- or lowercase or a mixture — IRC doesn't care.

The most important command for you to know gets you out of IRC:

```
/QUIT
```

The second most important command gives you an online summary of the various IRC commands:

/HELP

Here are a few of the most useful IRC commands:

Command	What It Does
/ADMIN *server*	Displays information about a server.
/AWAY	Enables you to tell IRC that you will be away for a while. You don't need to leave this type of message; if you do, however, it's displayed to anyone who wants to talk to you.
/CLEAR	Clears your screen.
/TIME	Displays the date and time in case you can't take your eyes off the screen for even a moment.
/TOPIC *whatweare-*	Sets the topic message for the current *talkingabout* channel.
/WHO *channel*	Lists all the people on *channel.* If you type /WHO *, you see displayed the names of the people on the channel you're on.

If anyone on IRC ever tells you to type commands you don't understand, *don't do it. Ever.* You can unwittingly give away control of your IRC program and even your computer account to another person that way.

Remember: Everything you type while you're on IRC goes out to the Internet, *except* lines that start with a slash (/).

If you use mIRC or Ircle, you can achieve most of the same effects controlled by IRC commands by choosing options from the menu bar or clicking icons on the toolbar. These IRC commands work too, however, and some IRC programs don't have menu bar or toolbar equivalents.

IRC channels

The most popular way to use IRC is through *channels.* Most channels have names that start with the # character. Channel names aren't case sensitive. Numbered channels also exist (when you type a channel number, don't use the # character).

Thousands of IRC channels are available. You can find an annotated list of some of the best by visiting www.funet.fi/~irc/ channels.html. Each channel listed there has its own linked home page that tells much more about what that channel offers. A searchable list of IRC channels is also available, at www.liszt.com/chat.

See also "Listing available channels," later in this part, to find out how to see a list of channels.

Good channels to know about include

- ✦ **#irchelp:** A place to ask questions about IRC. (Read the FAQ first: ***See also*** "Getting more info," later in this part.)

- ✦ **#newbies:** All your IRC questions answered.

- ✦ **#21plus:** and **#30plus:** Age-appropriate meeting places.

- ✦ **#41plus:** A more mature channel (many on it are younger).

- ✦ **#teens:** For teenagers — chill and chat.

- ✦ **#hottub:** A rougher meeting place.

- ✦ **#macintosh:** Mac users meet here.

- ✦ **#windows95:** Windows users meet here.

- ✦ **#chat:** A friendly chat channel.

- ✦ **#mirc:** A help channel for mIRC users.

Also, try # followed by the name of a country or major city.

Joining a channel

You join a channel by typing

`/JOIN #channelname`

To join the #dummies channel, for example, type **/join #dummies** and press Enter. Don't forget the / before the command or the # before the channel name.

In mIRC, you can click the Channel Folders button on the toolbar and then double-click one of the channels listed.

In Ircle, choose Command⇨Join.

After you join a channel, everything you type that doesn't start with a slash (/) appears on the screen of everyone on that channel after you press Enter. The text of your messages is preceded by your nickname.

Leaving a channel

You leave a channel by typing

`/LEAVE`

In mIRC, you can leave a channel by choosing the window for that channel.

In Ircle, choose Command⇨Part.

Listing available channels

In mIRC, click the List Channels button on the toolbar. If you're looking for a particular channel name, type in the Match text box the text you're looking for. If you want to see channels with at least several people in them (rather than the hundreds of channels with one bored, lonely, or lascivious person waiting in it), type a number in the min box. Then click Get List. The list of channels can be long, so displaying the list may take a few minutes. If you want to see the channels listed in your Channels folder (the list of channels you visit frequently), click the Channels folder button instead.

In Ircle, choose Command⇨List.

In other IRC programs, you can find out all the public and private channels by typing

```
/LIST
```

Before typing **/LIST**, type

```
/SET HOLD_MODE ON
```

This phrase keeps the names from flying by so fast onscreen that you can't read them. Don't forget to type **/SET HOLD_MODE OFF** after you finish reading the list.

You can also limit the number of channels listed by typing

```
/LIST -min 8
```

Only channels with at least eight people on them are listed when you type this phrase.

Pub means a public channel. You may also see Prv, which means a private channel. The @ sign indicates a channel operator *(chanop),* who is in charge of managing the goings-on of the channel.

Choosing an IRC nickname

Everyone using IRC needs a *nickname.* This name can be the same as the username in your e-mail address, although most people pick a different name. To choose a nickname, type

```
/NICK thenameyouwant
```

Nicknames can be as long as nine characters.

Unlike e-mail addresses, nicknames can change from day to day. Whoever claims a nickname first on an IRC server gets to keep it as long as she is logged in. Nicknames are good for only a single session on IRC. If you chatted with someone named ElvisPres yesterday and then run into someone named ElvisPres today, you have no guarantee that it's the same person.

If you use Ircle or mIRC, you can tell it your preferred nickname so that it doesn't ask you every time you run it:

✦ In Ircle, choose File⇨Preferences⇨Startup. Enter your name and then choose File⇨Save Preferences.

✦ In mIRC, choose File⇨Setup or press Alt+E and click the IRC Servers tab. mIRC lets you specify an alternative nickname too.

To find out more about the person behind a nickname, type

`/WHOIS nickname`

The two main ways to find out someone's nickname are to see it on a channel or have another user reveal it to you.

Holding a private conversation

To send a message to someone whose nickname you know, type

`/MSG nickname whatyouwanttosay`

This method becomes tiresome, however, for more than one or two lines of text. You can start a longer conversation instead by typing

`/QUERY nickname`

Now, whenever you type something that doesn't start with /, it appears on *nickname*'s screen, preceded by *your* nickname, immediately after you press Enter. (Well, sometimes a lag occurs.)

Starting your own channel

Each channel has its own channel operator, or *chanop,* who can control, to some extent, what happens on that channel. You can start your own channel and become its chanop by typing

`/JOIN #unusedchannelname`

As with nicknames, whoever asks for a channel name first gets it. You can keep the name for as long as you're logged on as the chanop. You can let other people be chanops for your channel; just make sure that they're people you can trust. A channel exists as long as anyone is in it; when the last person leaves, the channel winks out of existence.

Types of channels

Three types of channels are available in IRC:

✦ **Public:** Everyone can see them, and everyone can join.

✦ **Private:** Everyone can see them, and you can join them only by invitation.

✦ **Secret:** They do not show up in the / LIST command, and you can join them only by invitation.

If you're on a private or secret channel, you can invite someone else to join by typing

/INVITE nickname

If you get an invitation from someone on a private or secret channel and want to join, just type

/JOIN -INVITE

Some people like to write computer programs that sit on IRC channels and make comments from time to time. These programs are called *bots,* short for *robots.* Some people think that bots are cute; if you don't, just ignore them. (Our editor suggested an Unbelievable Weirdness icon for this paragraph.) A few fun bots have been sighted on channels on AnotherNet servers; we particularly enjoyed a bot that conducted a highly competitive anagram game.

Filing a complaint

Compared to AOL and CompuServe, IRC is a lawless frontier. Few rules, if any, exist. If things get really bad, you can try to find out the offender's e-mail address by using the /whois command — /whois badmother@iecc.com, for example. You can then send an e-mail complaint to the postmaster at the same host name; postmaster@iecc.com, in this case. Don't expect much help, however.

Getting more info

You can discover much more about IRC from these sources:

✦ **The official IRC home page in Finland:** www.funet.fi/~irc (where IRC was invented)

✦ **The New IRC user's page:** www.newircusers.com

✦ **The Usenet newsgroup:** alt.irc

✦ **The IRC FAQ:** www.irchelp.org

Web-Based Chat

A number of sites on the World Wide Web, including many portal sites, let you chat by using just your Web browser. Sometimes a Java applet is loaded automatically. Fewer people use Web-based chat than either America Online or IRC, although Web-based chat is becoming more popular. New chat sites appear all the time. You can find out more about these sites by starting at Yahoo (`www.yahoo.com`) and clicking Computers and Internet, Internet, World Wide Web, and Chat.

MUDs and MOOs

MUD, which originally stood for Multiple-User Dungeon, was a way for Internet users to play an online version of the fantasy role-playing game Dungeons and Dragons. MUDs have evolved from those beginnings, however, into a whole new way for people to interact electronically. The term *MUD* is now often said to stand for Multiple-User Dimension or Multiple-User Dialogue.

MOOs are an object-oriented version of MUDs. In a MOO, you not only interact with the other characters there but also can use a special programming language to create new things and even rooms in the imaginary world.

If chat is another culture, MUDs and MOOs are another solar system. You pick, rather than a nickname, an identity — a fantasy role you want to play in the MUD.

Many MUDs are based on the worlds created in popular films and novels, including *Star Wars, Star Trek,* J.R.R. Tolkien's *The Lord of the Rings,* Douglas Adams' *Hitchhikers' Guide to the Galaxy,* and especially Anne McCaffrey's *Dragonriders of Pern.*

Many MUDs are conflict-oriented with combat, battles, and even wars. Virtual death is a possible outcome. Don't say we didn't warn you.

Although MUDs and MOOs have their origins in fantasy games, they have also found serious uses as places for people with common professional interests to meet, hold discussions, take classes, and show off their latest accomplishments.

Using MUDs

Most MUDs are text-based, with no graphics. You type messages to the MUDs, such as "look around" or "pick up ax," and you get a message back. Different MUDs have different commands.

Most MUDs run on UNIX computers, and you generally access them by using telnet. (*See also* "Telnet" in Part X.)

People are now building virtual reality worlds on the Internet, where you see a three-dimensional landscape onscreen and your character and others are represented by 3-D figures that walk, talk, and gesture. One example is AlphaWorld, the largest of the 3-D communities that you can access using the Active Worlds 3-D browser. (See www.activeworlds.com to download the free browser and www.awcommunity.org for information about the 3-D worlds.)

Finding MUDs

Many MUDs are out there, each with its own personality. Here are some good places to look for one that may interest you:

+ **The MUD Resource Collection:** www.godlike.com/muds

+ **The MUD Connector:** www.mudconnect.com

A search for *MUDs* at Yahoo (www.yahoo.com) brings you to a large collection of MUD-related pages too. You can also find out more about MUDs by reading the newsgroups rec.games.mud.announce or alt.mud. The rec.games.mud hierarchy of Usenet newsgroups includes groups for each major type of MUD. Each newsgroup offers, of course, a FAQ for its type of MUD. We found this question in the FAQ for one group: "Is MUDing a game or an extension of real life with gamelike qualities?"

That should give you some idea of how devoted many MUDers are.

Getting started in MUDs

Here are some tips for getting into MUDs:

+ Read the MUD FAQ posted regularly to the newsgroup rec.games.mud.announce. The FAQ is also available from www.mudconnect.com/mudfaq.

+ Visit one of the MUD Web sites listed in the preceding section.

+ Pick a MUD that seems interesting to you.

+ Visit that MUD, read its help files, and try out its guest area, if it has one.

+ If the MUD you picked is based on a book or movie, read the book or see the movie. If you read the book or saw the movie a long time ago, read or see it again. These folks know the details.

+ Set aside a big block of time for yourself — a few hours at least — and plunge in.

Don't start MUDding during final exam week or just before that big presentation at work. One user reports that his first MUD adventure lasted 96 hours.

Internet Telephony

The Internet doesn't limit you to communication by typing. Today's powerful personal computers and fast modems let you send voice and even pictures over the Net. Best of all, no long-distance charges apply — even for calls overseas.

You do need a microphone or headset and either a fast PC with a sound card or a fast Mac, and your modem should be 28.8 Kbps or faster. You need the proper phone software, of course, although those packages cost less than a couple of months' worth of phone bills.

So why isn't everyone calling on the Internet yet? Here's the bad news:

+ Internet phone software is complicated to set up and use.

+ The sound quality is not that great at best and can be downright poor.

+ Both parties must have the equipment and have their computers turned on, which can be tricky to arrange.

+ Internet phone software may not work well if you're behind a firewall (if your computer is connected to a corporate LAN, for example).

+ Some packages require you to know the other person's IP address to make connections.

+ Different software packages often don't work with one another.

+ If Internet telephony is widely adopted, it will place a big strain on the Net and may raise the ire of phone regulators, especially in countries with state telephone monopolies.

Things will get better, though. The technology is improving all the time, with new features such as these:

+ **Whiteboards:** A special screen that both parties can see and draw on

+ **Text windows:** So that you can write notes that others can see, similar to online chat

+ **Conference calls:** Enables more than two people to talk together

✦ **Voice mail and voice e-mail:** For leaving a message at the beep.

✦ **Video phone:** Displays the other person's image onscreen in a small picture which changes at rates that can be as fast as several times per second

The adoption of standards such as ITU H.323 will let different software and computers talk to each other.

Although larger software companies (such as Microsoft, Netscape, Intel, and IBM —) are just entering the field, a number of Internet telephony packages are on the market now. Most offer a 30-day free trial.

Internet Phone (VocalTec)	www.vocaltec.com	Mac and Windows
Video Phone (Intel)	www.intel.com/product/videophone	Supports H.323 standard
NetMeeting (Microsoft)	www.microsoft.com/netmeeting	Comes with Windows 98
ClearPhone (Engineering Consulting)	www.clearphone.com	Uses QuickTime for high-quality Mac and Windows connections
DigiPhone (Wincroft, Inc.)	www.digiphone.co.uk	Mac and Windows 3.1, Windows 95, Windows 98, and Windows NT
Speak Freely	www.speakfreely.org	Open Source package offering something the others don't: encryption for real privacy; Windows and UNIX
Enhanced CU-SeeMe (White Pine Software)	www.cuseeme.com	Pioneering Internet video phone software

You can see up-to-date information about the fast-changing field of Internet telephony at

✦ **Voice on the Net:** www.von.com

✦ **Iphone:** www.pulver.com/iphone

✦ **Telirati:** www.phonezone.com/telirati

Part IX

Advanced Topics

This part talks about various Internet subjects you
don't need to think about right away. After you get
comfortable on the Net, however, you may want to consider these issues.

In this part . . .

- ✔ Encryption and Internet security
- ✔ Java and network computers
- ✔ Internet radio and television
- ✔ Your own Web home page
- ✔ Starting a Web business

Encryption and Internet Security

As your e-mail message or filled-out credit card form travels through the Internet, it passes through many different computers. Someone with the proper skills and equipment can intercept and read your message anywhere along the way without much trouble. This section describes methods people have developed for improving Internet and e-mail security.

Cryptography

A solution to the Internet's security problem is *cryptography* — the use of special computer programs to scramble data. Others cannot read the scrambled data unless they have the correct electronic key. *Keys* are short files of unique bits needed to unscramble messages. A file or message that has been deliberately scrambled by using cryptography is *encrypted*.

Traditional encryption systems, also called *symmetric key* systems, use the same key to encode and decode a message. Symmetric key systems can be quite simple — you can even find out how to build your own, at `ciphersaber.gurus.com` — although keeping track of the keys can be a challenge. All keys must be kept secret.

Public-key cryptography

Public-key cryptography, invented in the mid-1970s, simplifies encrypted communication by making it much easier to exchange keys. Public-key cryptography gives you two keys: one you keep secret (your *private key*) and another you can give to everyone (your *public key*). Here's how the concept works:

1. For two people (John and Arnold, for example) to communicate by using encrypted e-mail, each must first have a copy of the other's public key in his computer. (We tell you how that happens, in "Public-key infrastructure," later in this part.)

2. John encodes messages to Arnold by using Arnold's *public* key.

3. Arnold decodes John's messages by using Arnold's *private* key.

4. Arnold encodes his reply to John by using John's *public* key.

5. John decodes Arnold's reply by using John's *private* key.

No one ever needs to give anyone else a private key, yet everyone can communicate confidentially. Only Arnold can read the message that John sent to him, and only John can read Arnold's reply.

You can also use public-key cryptography to sign your messages in a way that cannot be forged — unless, of course, someone somehow manages to discover your private key. You encode part of your message by using your *private* key so that anyone can decode it with your *public* key. Because only you have access to your private key, only you could have encoded the message, so it must be from you.

The politics of cryptography

Cryptography is mired in hot political and legal controversy. Many governments around the world, including the U.S. government, wish that this technology had never been made available to the general public and are trying their best to control it:

+ The export of strong cryptographic software is illegal in the United States without a license.

+ An international arms control agreement called the Wassenaar Arrangement now bans the export of mass-market software containing strong cryptography.

+ The head of the U.S. Federal Bureau of Investigation (FBI) has called for a ban on the domestic distribution of any cryptographic software that blocks authorized government access to message content.

+ The U.S. government is working with computer companies to include ways to access keys without the user's knowledge. Pending legislation would make revealing these "back doors" a crime.

How secure is public-key cryptography?

Subject to several big "ifs," public-key cryptography is quite secure:

+ **If the program you use is carefully written.** Only careful scrutiny by cryptographic experts over an extended time, however, can determine just how carefully such a program is written. In 1995, for example, errors in the encryption code then used by Netscape enabled two graduate students, Ian Goldberg and David Wagner, to discover ways to break the Netscape code. Fortunately, those errors have now been fixed — and this kind of public review will, we hope, catch other errors quickly.

+ **If your key is long enough.** *See* the following section.

+ **If no breakthroughs occur in the mathematical knowledge needed to crack public keys.** Progress to-date has been slow but steady.

+ **If you can keep your private key secret.** Someone with the proper skills and access to your computer can steal your private key without your knowing it.

Key size

The security of public-key systems depends on the size of both the public key and the temporary symmetric keys these systems exchange every time they send a message.

Most experts recommend that symmetric keys be at least 80 bits long, preferably 128 bits. The U.S. government, however, prohibits the general export of software with symmetric keys larger than 56 bits. The difference between breaking a 56-bit and a 128-bit key is the difference between lifting a 200-pound weight and lifting Mt. Everest. Both Internet Explorer and Netscape Navigator are available in 128-bit versions for North American use and a 40-bit, 56-bit, or 64-bit version for export. Download the 128-bit version if you're in the United States or Canada; otherwise, visit `www.fortify.net`. *See also* "ABCs of the Web," in Part VI.

Some financial institutions wisely require the 128-bit version for online banking and trading.

Public keys are much longer than symmetric keys because they're the results of complicated mathematical operations. RSA Security (`www.rsasecurity.com`), the company that owns the patents on one type of public-key cryptography, recommends that your public key be at least this long:

+ **For personal use:** 768 bits

+ **For corporate use:** 1,024 bits

+ **For extremely valuable keys:** 2,048 bits

A 512-bit key, for many years the largest key size allowed for export, was broken by a European team in 1999.

Most people should use 1,024-bit public keys and 128-bit symmetric keys, if they're available.

Internet Explorer and Netscape Communicator

Internet Explorer and Netscape Communicator use public-key cryptography to let you send and receive encrypted information from special sites called *secure servers*. They use a version of public-key cryptography called *SSL*. This feature is particularly useful when you want to send your credit card number over the Net. These programs also allow you to encrypt e-mail.

Netscape Navigator 4.7 and Internet Explorer 5.0 show a closed lock icon in the lower-left corner of the screen if the connection is secure. If the lock is missing or is depicted as open, the connection is not secure. Netscape 3.0 shows a key icon in the lower-left corner of the screen for the same purpose.

Malicious individuals can hijack your connection and send you to their own, nonsecure site, just when a legitimate site is about to ask for your credit card number. Always look for the closed-lock icon in the lower-left corner of your browser window before giving out sensitive information!

Only the versions of Netscape Communicator and Internet Explorer (IE) offered in North America offer full security. The export and regular free versions have been deliberately weakened to comply with U.S. export regulations. (U.S. residents can download a full-security version of Netscape or IE only after affirming U.S. resident status.) If you cannot get the stronger version of Netscape, visit www.fortify.net.

Outlook Express and Netscape Messenger

Both Outlook Express, which comes with Windows 98 and MacOS 8.5, and Netscape Messenger, which comes with Netscape Communicator, allow you to send encrypted e-mail using public key cryptography.

✦ To encrypt a message with Outlook Express, click the envelope-with-a-lock icon in the New Message window. Click the envelope-with-a-seal icon to digitally sign a message.

Security

✦ To encrypt a message with Netscape Messenger, click the Security icon on the toolbar of the Message Composition window.

Before you can exchange messages with a friend, you each have to get keys from a certificate authority, such as VeriSign. *See* "Public-key infrastructure," later in this part.

Pretty Good Privacy

PGP, which stands for Pretty Good Privacy, is a freeware encryption program with a strong following on the Internet. Although others talk about e-mail security, PGP has been providing it for years. Here are some things you should know about this program:

✦ The latest version of PGP is available as a plug-in that adds encryption and electronic signatures to the menus of popular e-mail programs, including Eudora, Microsoft Exchange, Microsoft Outlook, and Claris Emailer.

✦ PGP supports two flavors of public-key cryptography: RSA and Diffie-Hellman (DH). Both are considered strong, although they use different mathematical algorithms.

✦ RSA is covered by a patent in the United States, and PGP has to pay royalties, but the Diffie-Hellman patents have expired. Therefore, the latest free PGP generates only Diffie-Hellman keys, although you can generate RSA keys with the older, freeware version of PGP, 2.6.2.

✦ You need to create separate keys for RSA and Diffie-Hellman if you want to communicate with users of both systems.

✦ Unlike VeriSign, PGP enables you to make your own public and private key pairs at no charge.

✦ The free versions PGP are for noncommercial use only.

✦ A version of PGP that supports both flavors of keys and permits commercial use is available in North America from PGP, Inc. Check the PGP Web page, at `www.pgp.com`. The full-strength international version is available at `www.pgpi.org`.

✦ Although the older, freeware version of PGP, 2.6.2, supports RSA keys, it's harder to use.

✦ Most experts consider PGP to be extremely secure if it's used correctly. In fact, PGP uses a signature scheme that is endorsed by the U.S. National Security Agency — strange bedfellows indeed.

Obtaining a copy of PGP

Getting your own copy of PGP is an adventure in itself.

The free version of PGP is distributed in the United States and Canada via the Massachusetts Institute of Technology PGP site:

`web.mit.edu/network/pgp.html`

Other parts of the world should visit the International PGP home page:

`www.pgpi.com`

You can purchase PGP from the PGP Division of Network Associates, at `www.pgp.com`.

No version of PGP is licensed for general export from the United States, but the United States does *not* regulate the export of printed books. PGP has therefore published its entire source code in book form, and volunteers outside the United States have prepared versions of free PGP from these books, which apparently makes PGP the only strong cryptographic software legally exported from the United States.

Getting started with PGP

Although the detailed commands are different in the various versions of PGP that are available, you have to perform the following steps to use PGP to communicate privately:

1. Obtain and install the PGP software.

2. Use your newly installed copy of PGP to check the signature on the copy of PGP you have just obtained.

3. Create a pass phrase for your private key. *See also* "Passwords and pass phrases," later in this part.

4. Use PGP to generate your own public and private keys.

5. Sign your key and, if possible, get other PGP users who know you to sign your key.

6. Post your public key to a key server so that others can easily find it.

7. Get the fingerprint of your key. The *fingerprint* is a short string of random-looking characters, derived from your key, that lets others be sure that they have a valid version of your key. For example, Arnold's PGP fingerprint is 031A340479 EA9E767B67, and John's is 3A5BD03FD9A06AA4 2DAC1E9EA636A347.

8. Get the public key of the person to whom you want to send a secret message, either in person on a floppy disk, from a key server or as an attachment to an unencoded e-mail message.

9. If you didn't get the key in person, verify its fingerprint with the recipient over the telephone (assuming that you can recognize her voice).

10. Encrypt your message and send it.

11. Decrypt any reply.

All these steps make the use of PGP seem somewhat complex — no one said that cryptography is simple. Still, to send more messages to the same recipient requires only the last two steps. Adding a new recipient involves only the last four steps.

For more information about PGP and related issues, visit Francis Litterio's Cryptography, PGP, and Your Privacy page:

```
world.std.com/~franl/crypto.html
```

You may also want to follow the Usenet newsgroups
alt.security.pgp and comp.security.pgp.discuss.

To read more about PGP, see *E-Mail For Dummies,* 2nd Edition, by John R. Levine, Carol Baroudi, Margaret Levine Young, and Arnold Reinhold (IDG Books Worldwide, Inc.).

HushMail

A new alternative to PGP is a web site named HushMail, at `www.hushmail.com`. HushMail is similar to other Web-based, advertising-supported, free e-mail sites, like HotMail or Yahoo, but with one very big difference: HushMail offers strong encryption.

HushMail uses public key encryption, but keeps your secret key on its server in encrypted form. This feature means that you can use HushMail from anywhere. Because HushMail utilizes the latest Java technology, you need a fairly recent browser to access its site.

Although HushMail is new and could have some unnoticed flaws, the designers seem committed to doing things the right way and have published the source code for the Java applet that performs encryption on your computer.

The biggest potential weakness in HushMail is that its security depends entirely on the pass phrase you select. We strongly recommend that you use a Diceware pass phrase of at least five words with HushMail. Six or seven words would be better. *See also* "Passwords and pass phrases," later in this part.

Remember that the secrecy of the message you send depends on your recipients' security measures, so encourage them to use a strong pass phrase as well.

Public-key infrastructure

Before public-key cryptography becomes widespread, Internet users need an easy way to get and verify someone's public key. One proposed method involves the creation of an international *public-key infrastructure* — a large hierarchy of organizations, sort of like the post office, that would issue keys to people. The infrastructure works like this:

+ Your key is signed by the office that issues it.

+ That office's key is signed by a higher office, and so on.

+ The top-level key is no doubt kept in a vault at the United Nations.

A number of companies are in the key-certifying business. Even the U.S. Postal Service is thinking of offering key certification.

One company that provides this service now is VeriSign, at
www.verisign.com. VeriSign calls its certified keys *Digital IDs*.
When you purchase a VeriSign Digital ID, you're covered by insurance against misuse.

✦ The Class 1 Digital ID that VeriSign sells to consumers ensures
only uniqueness of the owner's name and e-mail address. No
proof of identity is required to get one. Sometimes offered for
free with other software, a Class 1 certificate normally costs
about $15 per year and includes $1,000 of insurance coverage.

✦ A higher level of assurance, Class 3 requires verification and
physical appearance before an agent, such as a notary public,
is required. These certificates cost several hundred dollars per
year.

In what may be a record volume of fine print per dollar, the agree-
ments VeriSign asks you to accept to obtain an ID includes more
than 100 pages of legalese. In particular, VeriSign insurance does not
cover you if someone obtains your private key and you didn't take
reasonable measures to protect it, including keeping others from
using your computer without permission and using a good password.

PGP doesn't require a public-key infrastructure. Instead, PGP public
keys are distributed through a network of key servers and certified
via a method called "the Web of trust," which is kind of like the letters of introduction popular in the pre-electronic era. This approach
raises fewer civil liberties concerns than the public-key infrastructure needed by other systems.

Passwords and pass phrases

A first line of defense against someone's stealing your private key is
to use software, such as PGP, that encrypts your private key before
storing it. You choose a password or phrase that is used as the key
for this encryption. If you pick a pass phrase that is too easy to
guess (a single word will never do), the encryption can be broken.
For advice about picking a secure pass phrase, see the Diceware
page, at www.diceware.com.

Java and Network Computers

Java, developed by Sun Microsystems, is a programming language
intended to be a universal language for the Internet. Programs written in Java can run on almost any modern computer and operating
system, eliminating the need to develop, test, and distribute versions
of software for different computer platforms. For any programmer
types who have been isolated inside a cave for the past few years,
Java is an object-oriented language, somewhat like C but less
baroque than C++.

The universality of Java makes it a natural for distributing software over the Internet.

JavaScript is a scripting language for Web browsers. It can be extremely useful, although it shares nothing in common with Java other than the name and the marketing hype.

Java applets

A special subset of the Java language lets your browser safely download and run programs called *Java applets* that appear on Web pages. Limitations built into the browser are supposed to keep the applets from damaging anything on your computer, even if the author had malicious intent. At least, that's the theory.

In reality, Java applets aren't perfectly safe yet, although they're much less risky than other kinds of downloaded software.

To run Java applets, you must use a Java-enabled browser, such as Netscape Navigator 3.0 or Internet Explorer 3.0 or later versions of these programs.

Here are some key Java sites on the Web:

✦ **Sun Microsystems Java page:** www.sun.com/java

✦ **The official directory for Java:** With lots of applets; www.gamelan.com

In addition to the obvious coffee puns, the Java world is full of Indonesian double entendres.

Because two languages have Java in their names, you should check out three Dummies Press books to find out more: *Java For Dummies,* 3rd Edition, by Aaron E. Walsh; *Java Programming For Dummies,* 3rd Edition, by Donald and David Koosis; and *JavaScript For Dummies,* 2nd Edition, by Emily Vander Veer (all published by IDG Books Worldwide, Inc.).

Network computers

Because Java programs run on anything and are easy to download over networks, Java is a key technology in the *network computer* (or *NC*) concept. Network computers are simpler, smaller, and cheaper than personal computers and workstations because they don't have to store all their software locally — they get the software they need over the network when they need it. The big advantage for network computers may be that they're much easier and cheaper to support. NCs will appear in corporate offices soon, and maybe someday in homes.

Internet Radio and TV

Another new feature on the Internet is broadcasting. You can listen to live and recorded programming on your computer if you have

✦ **A fast modem:** One that's 28.8 Kbps or faster is recommended.

✦ **A PC:** Preferably a Pentium or faster, with a sound card, or a Macintosh, preferably a Power PC.

✦ **The proper browser plug-ins:** RealPlayer, for example, available at `www.real.com` (it has a free version and a more powerful cheap version). You also may want QuickTime, from `quicktime.apple.com`.

You can find out what radio and TV programs are available on the Web by visiting one of these sites:

✦ **On The Air, Inc.:** `www.ontheair.com`

✦ **RealGuide:** `www.real.com/realguide`

✦ **Yahoo! Broadcast:** `www.broadcast.com`

✦ **National Public Radio** has a extensive collection of past programs: `www.npr.org`

✦ **ThePublicRadioStation.com** is a 24-hour-a-day, Internet-based public radio station with programs from a variety of sources: `www.thepublicradiostation.com`

✦ **The Yahoo! collection of Internet broadcasting links:** `dir.yahoo.com/News_and_Media/Internet_Broadcasts/Radio`

Some broadcasts on the Internet contain more adult content than you would expect on regular radio stations.

Creating Your Own Web Home Page

With a little work, you can have your own, personal World Wide Web *home page* — a document that has its own URL and that can say anything you want it to. Most Internet service providers, including America Online and CompuServe, enable you to create and maintain a home page as part of your basic account; AOL even lets nonmembers make free pages (*see* "Creating a home page on America Online," later in this part). Other providers host your home page for a fee. GeoCities (`www.geocities.com`), Tripod (`www.tripod.com`), and many other companies offer free Web page hosting for noncommercial use.

Why would you want your own home page?

Here are some reasons to have a home page on the Web:

+ Advertise a business or hobby.

+ Start a new business. ***See also*** "Starting a Business on the Web," at the end of this part.

+ Help people find you more easily.

+ Publish your ideas and creations to the world.

+ Tell friends what's happening in your life (more than one pre-natal ultrasound image file is proudly displayed on the Internet).

+ Carve your initials on the Web as an art form or just for the fun of it.

You may also want to build a page to help an organization you belong to, such as a school, church, synagogue, mosque, or other charity.

Electronic commerce is exploding. A Web site for your business that at least lets the world know who you are, what you sell, and how to contact you is as vital as a listing in the phone book. While you're at it, reserve a domain name for your business. ***See also*** "Host names and domain names," in Part III.

If you ever saw the movie *Six Degrees of Separation,* you understand how easily a con artist can use a small amount of personal information about you to abuse your friends' and families' trust. A kidnapper who sees your kid's gymnastics award online could weave a convincing reason to pick her up early from class. Think before you put detailed personal information on your home page.

Building your page

Web pages are written in a special computer language called *HTML,* which stands for HyperText Markup Language. In this section, we tell you the basics of HTML.

A number of programs let you create HTML documents almost as easily as you create printed documents in a word processor. You don't have to understand HTML to use them, though we suggest skimming the following section anyway. ***See also*** "HTML editors," later in this part.

HTML files are usually stored with the extension `.html` or `.htm`. To create a simple page, you can write in the HTML language directly; it's not all that hard to do. Internet providers that support home pages offer HTML help files and sample pages you can use as a starting point.

Most users of personal computers are familiar with the *what you see is what you get* (or *WYSIWYG*) concept of document preparation. In using WYSIWYG, authors are in complete control of how their documents look. HTML, on the other hand, is based on a much different model. An author or an HTML editing program converts a text document into an HTML page by inserting *tags* that describe the function of various parts of the text, such as addresses, lists, headings, quotes, and words requiring emphasis.

HTML tags are code names surrounded by an open angle bracket (<) and a closed angle bracket (>). Some tags come in pairs enclosing some text; the starting tag in the pair appears at the beginning of the affected text, and the closing tag has a slash character (/) in its name. Text that appears between such pairs of tags is called *tagged text,* as shown in this example:

```
<B>This line appears in bold on your browser.</B>
```

The Web browser that reads the HTML page decides how tagged text appears onscreen. In particular, HTML ignores return characters and any extra spaces, except in preformatted text enclosed by the tags <PRE> and </PRE>.

The HTML concept is a throwback to 1970s text-preparation methods, although extensions have been added to HTML to give authors more control over the appearance of their pages. You need an HTML editor program to take full advantage of these extensions.

Most Web browsers enable you to read the HTML source text of any page you find interesting so that you can see how they do it. In Netscape Navigator, choose <u>V</u>iew⇨Document <u>S</u>ource or <u>V</u>iew⇨Page Source from the menu bar.

The following are some commonly used HTML tags:

<A> ... </A>	Indicates a *hypertext link*. For example:
	`<A href="http://net.gurus.com/">`
	`Cool help site!</a>`

<BLOCKQUOTE> ... </BLOCKQUOTE>	Displays enclosed text as indented block of text — typically used for a quotation from another source
 	Starts new line within a paragraph
<H*n*> ... </H*n*>	Indicates different heading levels, ranging in size from <H1> (largest) to <H6> (smallest)
<HR>	Draws line (a horizontal rule) across page
<LI>	Indicates item on a list
<OL> ... </OL>	Indicates ordered list; items in ordered list are typically numbered

(continued)

`<UL> ... </UL>`	Indicates unordered list; items in unordered list are typically bulleted
`<P>`	Indicates beginning of new paragraph
`<PRE> ... </PRE>`	Displays enclosed text as is, using its native spacing and line breaks; a monospace font is normally used, making `<PRE>` ideal for displaying tables or ASCII art (pictures drawn in characters)
`<EM> ... </EM>`	Emphasizes enclosed text, typically by displaying it with <u>underlining</u>
`<STRONG> ... </STRONG>`	Displays enclosed text in strong emphasis style — typically in **boldface** type
`<I> ... </I>`	Displays enclosed text in *italicized* style
`<B> ... </B>`	Displays enclosed text in **boldface** style
`<TT> ... </TT>`	Displays enclosed text as typewriter text, typically shown in `monospace` font
`<META> ... </META>`	Encloses text addressed to any indexer program; text is not displayed on your page
`<TABLE> ... </TABLE>`	With additional tags in between, defines a table; don't even *think* of using tables without a good HTML editor

Before you begin your page in earnest, make yourself a sampler — an HTML document in which you try out all the tags you want to use.

Tips for effective Web pages

Your Web page is more effective if you follow these guidelines:

+ Spend hours surfing the Web, and take notes as you go. Imitate the sites you admire.

+ Content counts. Provide solid information, interesting artwork, entertaining stories, well-maintained links, or something else to make a visit worthwhile.

+ Make your point at the beginning of the first page. Most visitors spend less than ten seconds at your site unless you grab their interest.

+ Get an easy-to-remember URL (no, they aren't all taken) and consider registering it as a trademark.

+ Focus on the essentials. Keep it simple.

+ Don't let backgrounds and font colors interfere with legibility. Black text on a white background is always in good taste.

+ Use color and graphics judiciously. They should enhance your message, not make your site harder to read.

✦ Avoid Web clichés, such as Under Constructions signs and animated images that distract visitors from your message.

✦ Design every page for indexing. Include all key words in the first paragraph or two and use the <META> tag. *See also* "META tags," later in this part.

✦ Make sure that visitors have something to read while they wait for any graphics to appear on their screens.

✦ Secondary pages should have an explicit link to your main page. If visitors get to the secondary page via a link from an indexer, their browsers' Back buttons won't get them to your main page.

✦ Make your site text-friendly. Some visitors cannot use graphics — either because of disability or having an older computer.

✦ Respect copyrights. Follow the golden rule.

✦ Most Web users connect to the Net through a modem. Make the loading of large image files optional.

✦ Test your site by using a 14.4 Kbps modem — the slowest in common use.

✦ Check how your page looks on both Netscape Navigator, Internet Explorer, and WebTV. The page displays on these programs can differ greatly!

✦ If you want people to visit your page, get it indexed at as many appropriate sites as you can. *See also* "Publicizing your page," later in this part.

✦ Stay put. Links to your site are priceless. Don't break those links by changing the URL of your Web pages unless absolutely necessary, and provide a cross-reference from the old URL if you do change.

✦ If you want visitors to come back again, you must give them a compelling reason to do so. The Web contains many sites to see.

Web page maintenance

Creating your Web page is only half the job. It gets stale in a hurry if you don't maintain it. Here are some tips:

✦ Check all your links regularly by clicking them and seeing whether they still go where they should. Update or delete any that go nowhere. Look at the Web shareware sites for programs that do this automatically. For example, Alert LinkRunner for Windows (www.alertbookmarks.com/lr) checks the links within your site and out to the Web.

✦ Link to the main page of sites wherever possible. Although Webmasters rearrange the content within a site regularly, top-level addresses don't change as often. For example, link to `net.gurus.com` rather than `net.gurus.com/toc-idq6.html`.

✦ Some large sites suggest safe ways for you to link to individual pages.

✦ Isolate in a separate page with a simple, easy-to-update format any information that changes regularly.

✦ Every now and then, ask someone else to find and tour your site while you watch.

✦ Make yourself a maintenance checklist and schedule that you're willing to follow. A low-maintenance page containing a mission description and contact information — with no time-dependent information and few or no links — is better for an organization than is a complex page filled with expired links and announcements for events that have already happened.

✦ Include an e-mail address in your page and invite comments and suggestions.

HTML editors

A number of excellent commercial HTML editors are on the market, and they're well worth the investment if you plan to do much Web publishing. An HTML editor named Composer is built into Netscape Communicator 4.0 and later versions. Windows 98 comes with an editor named FrontPage Express.

Several shareware HTML editors are also available on the Net. Good examples include

✦ **Hot Dog Web Editor (Windows), by Sausage Software:** `www.sausage.com`

✦ **BBEdit Lite (Macintosh), by Bare Bones Software, Inc.:** `www.barebones.com`

Microsoft Word can create and edit Web pages, and it even comes with a wizard to help you do so. WordPerfect 8 can also edit Web pages.

Most Web browsers let you display your home page HTML file so that you can see how it will appear on the Web. In Netscape Navigator or Internet Explorer, choose File⇨Open Page (or just Open) from the menu bar.

An excellent compendium of HTML elements by Ron Woodall is at `www.htmlcompendium.org`.

Creating a home page on America Online

AOL members can have a home page at no additional cost. Each screen name under your account can store as much as 12 megabytes of Web information, enough for fairly complex pages if you don't use a number of large graphics or multimedia files.

To find the home page (if he has one) of a member named *screen name,* point your browser to

hometown.aol.com/*screenname*

Note: Some AOL Web pages may be stored under members.aol. com/screenname.

You can use any HTML editor to create a home page and then upload the HTML file to AOL, although AOL also provides a novice-friendly Web page authoring tool named 1-2-3 Publish. Click My AOL on the toolbar and choose My Web Page from the menu that appears or type the keyword **personal publisher**.

A page created using 1-2-3 Publish can be edited by using any HTML editor; after you have changed the page in this way, however, you can no longer edit it with 1-2-3 Publish.

Publicizing your page

If you want people to visit your page, you have to let them know about it.

Almost all the Web search sites and directories let you register your page with them — look for a button that says something like Add URL. Some search sites need only your URL, and others have you fill out a form that requests your site's name, location, and keywords and a short description.

You can save yourself a great deal of surfing by using a Web site *submittal service.* Although these services used to be free, most now charge a fee. Here are a few:

+ **Submit It:** www.submit-it.com (limited, although useful parts are still free — look for the Free Trial link)

+ **Go Net-Wide:** www.GoNetWide.com/gopublic.html

+ **WebPromote:** www.usaworld.com/WebPromote.htm

You can find many more listed at Yahoo! (www.yahoo.com): Click Computers and Internet, Internet, World Wide Web, and then Announcement Services.

After you fill out the submittal services form and click the Submit button, you have to wait as each site is contacted and gets confirmation. This process takes awhile, so be patient and don't interrupt the process.

Yahoo (at www.yahoo.com) is one of the better Web directories, in part because humans review all submissions. You have to follow the Yahoo submittal instructions carefully if you want to be listed there.

Link exchanges and Webrings

You may be able to exchange links with other sites that have similar themes. For more information, visit www.linkexchange.com.

Webrings are groups of Web sites that link to each other to form a circle in cyberspace. Visit www.webring.com for information about more than 15,000 Webrings you can join or to find out how to start your own ring.

META tags

Some Web indexers (such as AltaVista) don't ask for keywords and descriptions when you register with them. Instead, these sites get all the information they need from your pages, indexing all the words and using the first sentence or two as a page description. In fact, these indexers visit your page regularly to update their listings.

You can control how these sites index your pages by including a META tag in the HEAD section of each page you make. Most indexers use the description you provide in the META tag and add any included keywords to those it got from your page's text. A page about this book, for example, may contain

```
<META name="description"
content="A compact, inexpensive, easy to understand
    guide to the Internet.">

<META name="keywords" content="book, reference,
    world wide Web, www, w3, internet, e-mail,
    email, dummies, dummy, dumby, beginner, novice,
    newbie, computer phobic">
```

Include keywords that may not be in the main text, variant spellings, and even common misspellings. You want people to find you, even if they spell a keyword wrong.

So many sites have abused META tags — including sensational, unrelated words, for example, or the product names of competitors — that many indexers no longer rely on them.

Starting a Business on the Web

Turning a clever idea into a billion-dollar online venture is the latest fad. Everyone else is doing it, so why not give it a try? At the worst, you will lose your home, savings, spouse, and several years of your life, but you will receive a valuable education in the process.

If we haven't put you off, you may have what it takes to start a Web business. Here are some tips:

✦ Spend a long time searching the Web for potential competitors and studying successful online businesses that you want to emulate.

✦ Focus on your *value proposition:* Why should customers buy from you, and why will they feel so good about their purchase that they tell their friends?

✦ Make sure that you like your product. You will be spending most waking hours on it.

✦ Find a good lawyer and a good accountant (not your in-laws).

✦ Get an easy-to-remember domain name in the .com zone. Avoid tricky spelling and punctuation. In traditional business, location is everything. On the Web, your domain name *is* your location.

✦ Follow the tips on Web page design and publicity in the preceding section.

✦ You will have to accept credit cards, a complex and expensive undertaking. Visit your bank or acceptance sites, such as www.charge.com. (See what we mean about memorable domain names?)

✦ Amazon.com's zStores offer a simple and inexpensive alternative for online credit card payment. *See* payments.amazon.com.

✦ If you plan to sell software you have written, check out www.kagi.com.

✦ Make sure that your site is easy to use. Customers should be able to complete the most common purchase in a few clicks.

✦ Learn about marketing. Creating a Web-based store on the Internet isn't that hard, although getting people to visit it can be. Think of the World Wide Web as one big shopping mall. It has room for only a few successful stores in any given category. How will you stand out?

✦ Plan for success. You must be ready to build online and offline capacity fast if your business takes off. (***Hint:*** It takes money and good people. Do you know where to find them?)

✦ Think about international aspects of your business, language localization, delivery, customs and payment problems, and possible partners.

✦ If you don't have a background in business, get one. Many business schools offer night courses for budding entrepreneurs. (If you cannot explain *cash flow, working capital, product positioning,* and *surge capacity,* we're talking to you.)

For more information about Web business topics, see the following books, all published by IDG Books Worldwide, Inc.:

✦ *Accounting For Dummies,* by John A. Tracy

✦ *Business Plans For Dummies,* by Paul Tiffany and Steven D. Peterson

✦ *Customer Service For Dummies,* 2nd Edition, by Karen Leland and Keith Bailey

✦ *HTML for Dummies,* 3rd Edition, by Ed Tittel and Stephen N. James

✦ *Managing For Dummies,* by Bob Nelson and Peter Economy

✦ *Marketing Online For Dummies,* by Bud Smith and Frank Catalano

✦ *Negotiating For Dummies,* by Michael C. Donaldson and Mimi Donaldson

✦ *Selling Online For Dummies,* by Leslie Heeter Lundquist

✦ *Small Business For Dummies,* by Eric Tyson and Jim Schell

✦ *Time Management For Dummies,* 2nd Edition, by Jeffrey J. Mayer

Part X

Classic Internet

Although e-mail and the World Wide Web dominate Internet use today, the Internet was originally built up from a number of smaller tools that were part of the UNIX operating system. The functions of many of these tools are now performed by Web browsers, such as Netscape Navigator and Microsoft Internet Explorer. You may have to use these tools directly from time to time, however, and understanding how they work helps you use your browser more effectively. We tell you a little about them in this part.

In this part . . .

- ✓ **FTP, for file transfers**
- ✓ **Telnet, for logging in to computers as a terminal**
- ✓ **A quick guide to UNIX and Linux commands**
- ✓ **Finger, for getting information about host computers and people**

FTP

The Internet copies files between your computer and other computers on the Internet by using a facility known as FTP *(File Transfer Protocol).* You connect your computer to an *FTP server,* an Internet host computer that stores files for transfer. Many publicly accessible FTP servers enable you to log in and retrieve a wide variety of files, including software, text files, and graphics files. On these systems, rather than log in with your own name and password, you log in as **anonymous** and use your e-mail address or the word *guest* as the password.

Your browser can usually log in as anonymous for you, download the file you want, log off, and unpack the file — all automatically. URLs that start with ftp:// take you to an FTP site.

When you transfer a file by using any FTP program, the program has to know whether the file contains text or anything else. If the file contains only text, it transfers the file in ASCII mode; otherwise, it uses Binary or Image mode. Some FTP programs can look at the file you want to transfer and guess the mode; other programs require you to specify.

Using FTP programs

Sometimes, you may want more control over the file-transfer process — for example, when you're uploading files to a remote Web server. If you use a PPP account, you can use Winsock or Macintosh TCP/IP-compatible software to move files on the Internet:

+ **WS_FTP LE for Windows:** From Ipswitch, Inc., and available at http://www.ipswitch.com

+ **Fetch for Macintosh:** Written by Jim Mathees and available at http://www.dartmouth.edu/pages/softdev/fetch.html

Both programs are also available from the shareware sources listed in Part VII.

On America Online and CompuServe, go to keyword **ftp**.

On UNIX systems, type **ftp** followed by the host name of the server. Type your login name and password for that server when you're asked.

Navigating files and directories

Most Winsock and Mac TCP/IP programs use a full-screen interface that displays in one window the files in the current directory on the FTP server (the *remote* system) and in another window the files on your own computer (the *local* system). Before you can transfer files, you want to display in one window the files to transfer and in the other window the directory you want to transfer them to.

To change directories, click the name of the directory you want to move to in the FTP window. If you want to move to the parent directory of the current directory, click the **..** entry on the directory list.

UNIX users give FTP commands similar to the ones they would use for local file management. To change to a directory, for example, you type **cd** followed by the name of the directory. To see a list of the files in a directory, type **dir**. To move to the parent directory of the current directory, type the **cd ..** command.

Uploading and downloading files

If you use an FTP program with a full-screen interface (such as WS_FTP), click all the names of the files you want to transmit. Click the ASCII button if the files contain only text, or the Binary button otherwise. Then click the transfer button that points from the system where the files are to the system on which you want them.

UNIX users, type the **ascii** command if the files to be transferred contain only text, or the **image** or **binary** command if they contain something other than text. To download a file from the other computer to your computer, type the **get** command followed by the name of the file. To upload a file from your computer to the other computer, type **put** followed by the name of the file.

When you're done copying files, disconnect from the FTP server.

✦ If you're using a graphics FTP program, click the Disconnect button or choose Disconnect from the menu.

✦ If you're using the UNIX FTP program, type **quit**.

Telnet

Telnet enables you to log in to other computers on the Net as though you were connected to them directly. Don't worry — it's perfectly legal! Telnet works only if the other computer gives permission. A major use of telnet these days is connecting to MUDs (*see also* the section in Part VIII about MUDs and MOOs.).

Using telnet from a Winsock or MacTCP program

If you use a PPP account or a direct Internet connection, you can use a Winsock or Macintosh TCP/IP-compatible telnet program, such as

✦ **Telnet:** The program that comes with Windows 95 and Windows 98

✦ **NetTerm for Windows:** From InterSoft International, Inc., and available at `http://starbase.neosoft.com/~zkrr01`.

✦ **Better Telnet for Macintosh:** Visit `www.cstone.net/~rbraun/mac/telnet` for a copy.

Both programs are also available from the shareware sources listed in Part VII.

Winsock and Mac TCP/IP telnet programs use a graphical interface that includes a window in which you type commands and see the remote computer's responses.

If you're using a Web browser (such as Netscape or Internet Explorer) and want to telnet to some site — `foo.com`, for example — try sending your browser to the URL `telnet://foo.com`.

Connecting to remote computers

On windowing systems, you type the host name in a pop-up window after choosing Connect or Open Connection from the menu bar.

On UNIX systems, you type **telnet** followed by the host name of the computer you want to log in to. (Type **tn3270** instead to connect to older IBM mainframes.)

To access remote computers from CompuServe, go to keyword **telnet**.

The remote system usually asks you to enter your username *on that system* and then your password. You may be asked what kind of terminal you're using (common terminal types include VT100, ANSI, and 3101). If you indicate the wrong type, the information on your screen may be scrambled. If telnet suggests a terminal type, accept it and see what happens.

Disconnecting from remote computers

You end a telnet session by typing **logout**, **exit**, or **bye** or pressing Ctrl+D or Ctrl+] (that's the Control key and then the right bracket).

On windowing systems, just close the telnet window.

UNIX and Linux commands

Telnet may bring you to one of the many UNIX or Linux systems on the Internet. Here's a brief guide to some of the most important UNIX and Linux commands:

`cd` *directoryname*	Changes the current directory.
`cd ..`	Brings you up one directory level.
`cd`	Returns you to your home directory.
`Control-C`	Terminates most operations.
`cp` *filename1 filename2*	Copies a file.
`logout`	Terminates your session.
`ls`	Lists the files in the current directory. For more complete information, use `ls -alF`.
`man` *commandname*	Displays a page of instructions for that command; for example, `man ls`.
`mkdir` *newdirectoryname*	Makes a new directory.
`more` *filename*	Displays a text file one page at a time. Press the spacebar to see the next page; press Q to quit.
`mv` *filename1 filename2*	Moves a file or changes its name.
`pwd`	Prints the current working directory.
`rm` *filename*	Deletes a file. ***Caution:*** UNIX, unlike Windows and MacOS, doesn't have a way to undo a file deletion.
`rmdir` *directoryname*	Removes an empty directory.

UNIX filenames are similar to Windows 98 filenames, except that UNIX uses forward slashes (/) rather than backslashes (\). You can use an asterisk (*) as a wildcard in a filename in most commands. Filenames that start with a period (.) are normally hidden and are used to store the settings for various programs.

The tilde character (~) is used as an abbreviation for a home directory path: `cd ~` takes you to your home directory, and `cd ~arnold` takes you to Arnold's home directory.

For more information about using UNIX tools, buy a copy of *UNIX For Dummies,* 3rd Edition, written by John R. Levine and Margaret Levine Young (IDG Books Worldwide, Inc.).

Finger

You can check up on people using UNIX computers on the Net by using finger.

On UNIX systems, type **finger** followed by the user's name and then an at-sign (@) followed by the host computer's name on the command line, as in

`finger johnl@gurus.com`

On Macs and Windows machines, start the finger program, available from the shareware sources listed in Part VII, and then enter the person's e-mail address in the appropriate fields.

On UNIX systems, you can store in a special text file named `.plan` the information you want displayed when someone "fingers" your account.

Internet Country Codes

This appendix lists the two-letter country codes found at the end of Internet e-mail addresses and World Wide Web domain names. Countries are listed in alphabetical order by country code. The codes are based on, for the most part, an international standard named ISO-3166. If you're curious about a country on this list, look up the country in the CIA's *World Factbook,* at www.odci.gov/cia/publications/factbook.

Note that some countries — such as Niue (.nu), Turkmenistan (.tm), Tonga (.to), Tuvalu (.tv), and Uzbekistan (.uz) — are selling vanity domain names to sites outside those countries. Every country domain is active except for iq (Iraq) and kp (North Korea.) Some "countries" are uninhabited territories, such as tf and gs, which are managed by someone in the country that owns the territory and are invariably used as vanity domains.

See Part III to find the traditional 3-letter global top-level domain names .com, .edu, .gov, .int, .mil, .net, and .org and some proposed new global names.

Code	Country
AD	Andorra
AE	United Arab Emirates
AF	Afghanistan
AG	Antigua and Barbuda
AI	Anguilla
AL	Albania
AM	Armenia
AN	Netherlands Antilles
AO	Angola
AQ	Antarctica
AR	Argentina
AS	American Samoa
AT	Austria
AU	Australia
AW	Aruba
AZ	Azerbaijan
BA	Bosnia and Herzegovina
BB	Barbados
BD	Bangladesh
BE	Belgium
BF	Burkina Faso
BG	Bulgaria
BH	Bahrain
BI	Burundi
BJ	Benin
BM	Bermuda
BN	Brunei Darussalam
BO	Bolivia
BR	Brazil
BS	Bahamas
BT	Bhutan
BV	Bouvet Island
BW	Botswana
BY	Belarus
BZ	Belize

Code	Country
CA	Canada
CC	Cocos (Keeling) Islands
CD	Congo-Kinshasa (formerly Zaire)
CF	Central African Republic
CG	Congo-Brazzaville
CH	Switzerland
CI	Côte d'Ivoire
CK	Cook Islands
CL	Chile
CM	Cameroon
CN	China
CO	Colombia
CR	Costa Rica
CU	Cuba
CV	Cape Verde
CX	Christmas Island
CY	Cyprus
CZ	Czech Republic
DE	Germany
DJ	Djibouti
DK	Denmark
DM	Dominica
DO	Dominican Republic
DZ	Algeria
EC	Ecuador
EE	Estonia
EG	Egypt
EH	Western Sahara
ER	Eritrea
ES	Spain
ET	Ethiopia
FI	Finland
FJ	Fiji
FK	Falkland Islands (Malvinas)

Code	Country
FM	Micronesia
FO	Faroe Islands
FR	France
GA	Gabon
GD	Grenada
GE	Georgia
GF	French Guiana
GH	Ghana
GI	Gibraltar
GL	Greenland
GM	Gambia
GN	Guinea
GP	Guadeloupe
GQ	Equatorial Guinea
GR	Greece
GS	South Georgia and the South Sandwich Islands
GT	Guatemala
GU	Guam
GW	Guinea-Bissau
GY	Guyana
HK	Hong Kong
HM	Heard Island and Mcdonald Islands
HN	Honduras
HR	Croatia
HT	Haiti
HU	Hungary
ID	Indonesia
IE	Ireland
IL	Israel
IN	India
IO	British Indian Ocean Territory
IQ	Iraq
IR	Iran

Code	Country
IS	Iceland
IT	Italy
JM	Jamaica
JO	Jordan
JP	Japan
KE	Kenya
KG	Kyrgyzstan
KH	Cambodia
KI	Kiribati
KM	Comoros
KN	Saint Kitts and Nevis
KP	North Korea
KR	South Korea
KW	Kuwait
KY	Cayman Islands
KZ	Kazakstan
LA	Laos
LB	Lebanon
LC	Saint Lucia
LI	Liechtenstein
LK	Sri Lanka
LR	Liberia
LS	Lesotho
LT	Lithuania
LU	Luxembourg
LV	Latvia
LY	Libya
MA	Morocco
MC	Monaco
MD	Moldova
MG	Madagascar
MH	Marshall Islands
MK	Macedonia
ML	Mali
MM	Myanmar

Code	Country
MN	Mongolia
MO	Macau
MP	Northern Mariana Islands
MQ	Martinique
MR	Mauritania
MS	Montserrat
MT	Malta
MU	Mauritius
MV	Maldives
MW	Malawi
MX	Mexico
MY	Malaysia
MZ	Mozambique
NA	Namibia
NC	New Caledonia
NE	Niger
NF	Norfolk Island
NG	Nigeria
NI	Nicaragua
NL	Netherlands
NO	Norway
NP	Nepal
NR	Nauru
NU	Niue
NZ	New Zealand
OM	Oman
PA	Panama
PE	Peru
PF	French Polynesia
PG	Papua New Guinea
PH	Philippines
PK	Pakistan
PL	Poland
PM	Saint Pierre and Miquelon
PN	Pitcairn

Code	Country
PR	Puerto Rico
PS	Palestinian Territory
PT	Portugal
PW	Palau
PY	Paraguay
QA	Qatar
RE	Réunion
RO	Romania
RU	Russia
RW	Rwanda
SA	Saudi Arabia
SB	Solomon Islands
SC	Seychelles
SD	Sudan
SE	Sweden
SG	Singapore
SH	Saint Helena
SI	Slovenia
SJ	Svalbard and Jan Mayen
SK	Slovakia
SL	Sierra Leone
SM	San Marino
SN	Senegal
SO	Somalia
SR	Suriname
ST	Saõ Tóme and Principe
SU	Soviet Union (still in use)
SV	El Salvador
SY	Syrian Arab Republic
SZ	Swaziland
TC	Turks and Caicos Islands
TD	Chad
TF	French Southern Territories
TG	Togo
TH	Thailand

Code	Country
TJ	Tajikistan
TK	Tokelau
TM	Turkmenistan
TN	Tunisia
TO	Tonga
TP	East Timor
TR	Turkey
TT	Trinidad and Tobago
TV	Tuvalu
TW	Taiwan
TZ	Tanzania
UA	Ukraine
UG	Uganda
UK	United Kingdom
UM	United States Minor Outlying Islands
US	United States
UY	Uruguay
UZ	Uzbekistan
VA	Vatican City
VC	Saint Vincent and The Grenadines
VE	Venezuela
VG	Virgin Islands, British
VI	Virgin Islands, U.S.
VN	Vietnam
VU	Vanuatu
WF	Wallis and Futuna
WS	Samoa
YE	Yemen
YT	Mayotte
YU	Yugoslavia
ZA	South Africa
ZM	Zambia
ZW	Zimbabwe

Techie Talk

Terms that are defined elsewhere in this glossary are generally shown in ***bold italics.***

10BaseT: A way of distributing ***Ethernet*** data short distances over ordinary phone wiring. 100BaseT is the same idea, but faster.

ActiveX: A Microsoft standard for computer program building blocks, known as ***objects.***

ADSL: Asymmetric Digital Subscriber Line, a technology that lets you transmit data over phone lines faster — as much as 8 million bps — in one direction than in the other. Also just DSL.

AES: Advanced Encryption Standard, the U.S. government's planned replacement for ***DES.***

AltaVista: An excellent World Wide Web search engine, at `www.altavista.com`.

America Online (AOL): A value-added online service that provides many services in addition to Internet access, including access to popular chat groups.

anonymous FTP: A way of using the FTP program to log on to another computer to copy files, even though you don't have an account on the other computer. When you log on, you type anony-mous as the username and your e-mail address as the password.

applet: A small computer program written in the Java programming language. You can download applets by using a Web ***browser.*** Applets must obey special rules that make it difficult for the programs to do damage to your computer.

archive: A single file containing a group of files that have been compressed and glommed together for efficient storage. You have to use a program such as PKUNZIP, StuffIt, tar, or WinZip to get the original files back out.

ARPANET: The original ancestor of the Internet, funded by the U.S. Department of Defense.

ASCII: American Standard Code for Information Interchange, the way most computers store ***text files.***

attachment: A computer file electronically stapled to an e-mail message and sent along with it.

AUP: Acceptable-use policy. Guidelines a company or school issues that specify inappropriate uses of their Internet connection. (If you have to ask, it's probably a no-no.)

baud: The number of electrical symbols per second that a modem sends down a phone line. Often used as a synonym for bps (bits per second). This usage is incorrect, but only 43 people on the entire planet know why or care. Named after J. M. E. Baudot, the inventor of the Teletype.

BBS: *B*ulletin *b*oard *s*ystem, an electronic-message system you dial up directly to read and post messages. Most have been replaced by the Internet.

Bcc: *B*lind *c*arbon *c*opy. Bcc addressees get a copy of your e-mail without other recipients knowing about it. Considered sneaky, but okay for long mailing lists. ***See also*** Cc.

binary file: A file which contains information that does not consist only of text. For example, a binary file may contain an archive, a program, a picture, sounds, a spreadsheet, or a word-processing document that includes formatting codes in addition to characters.

BinHex: A file-encoding system popular among Macintosh users.

bit: The smallest unit of measure for computer data. Bits can be *on* or *off* (symbolized by 1 or 0) and are used in various combinations to represent different kinds of information.

BITNET: An older network of large computers connected to the Internet.

bookmark: The address (URL) of a Web page you may want to see again. In Netscape, you store URLs in a bookmark file. Internet Explorer stores bookmarks in the Favorites folder.

bounce: To return as undeliverable. If you mail a message to a bad address, it bounces back to your mailbox.

bps: *B*its *p*er *s*econd, a measure of how fast data is transmitted. Often used to describe modem speed.

broadband: A technology for sending multiple channels of information over a coaxial or fiber-optic cable. Used with cable modems.

browser: A superduper, all-singing, all-dancing program that lets you read information on the World Wide Web. *See also* Part VI.

byte: A group of eight bits. Computer memory is usually measured in bytes.

Cc: *C*arbon *c*opy, or *c*ourtesy *c*opy. Cc addressees get a copy of your e-mail, and other recipients are informed of it if they bother to read the message header. *See also* Bcc.

CCITT: The old name for *ITU-T,* a United Nations committee that sets worldwide communication standards.

CGI script: A language used on Web servers to process user forms and other user requests.

channel: In IRC, a group of people chatting together. America Online and CompuServe call channels *rooms* (*see also* Part VIII). Value-added providers use *channel* to refer to a major interest area you can get to easily, like a TV channel.

chanop: In IRC, the *chan*nel *op*erator is the person in charge of keeping order in a channel. The chanop can throw out unruly visitors. *See also* Part VII.

chat: To talk live to other network users from any and all parts of the world. To chat on the Internet, you use Internet Relay Chat (IRC). America Online, CompuServe, and Delphi have similar services. *See also* Part VIII.

client: A computer that uses the services of another computer, or *server.* If you dial in to another system, your computer becomes a client of the system you dial in to (unless you're using X Windows — don't ask).

CompuServe (CIS): A value-added online service that provides many services in addition to Internet access, including forums for many popular business topics.

cookie: A small text file, stored on your hard disk by a Web site you have visited, that contains information to remind the site about you the next time you visit it.

country code: The last part of a geographic address, which indicates in which country the host computer is located, such as us for the United States. The country abbreviations originate from *ISO* standard 3166. For a complete list, see the appendix.

CyberPatrol: A program that tries to keep kiddies from accessing Web sites the company deems inappropriate.

DejaNews: A Web service that stores and indexes all *newsgroup* messages. *See also* Part IV.

DES: Data Encryption Standard, a U.S. government standard for encrypting unclassified data. Breakable at some expense, although a newer version, triple-DES, is probably safe.

Dial-Up Networking: The Internet communications program that comes with Windows 95 and Windows 98.

Diffie-Hellman (D-H): An algorithm for *public-key cryptography* that's popular because its patent has expired. *See also* Part IX.

digest: A compilation of the messages that have been posted to a mailing list during the past few days.

domain: Part of the official name of a computer on the Net — for example, iecc.com. To find out how to register a domain name, *see* Part III.

domain name server (DNS): A computer on the Internet that translates between Internet domain names, such as xuxa.iecc.com, and Internet numerical addresses, such as 140.186.81.2. Sometimes just called *name server.* When a *browser* complains that a *URL* is not in the DNS, it often means that the server just took too long to respond. If you think that the name is right, try it again.

download: To copy a file from a remote computer "down" to your computer.

DSL: Digital Subscriber Line. *See* ADSL.

dummies: People who don't know everything but are smart enough to seek help. Used ironically.

duplex: Able to send information in both directions. Just say "full" when you're setting up a communications program.

e-mail: Messages sent electronically, usually over the Internet. *See also* Part III.

Ethernet: A fast Local-Area Network developed by Xerox.

Eudora: A popular mail-handling program that runs on the Macintosh and under Windows. *See also* Part III.

FAQ: Frequently Asked Questions, a collection of answers to questions that come up in online discussions or that the person who compiles them thinks ought to come up. Many newsgroups have FAQs that are posted regularly. To read the FAQs for all newsgroups, FTP to rtfm.mit.edu or search on *topic* FAQ at deja.com.

Favorites: A list of Web sites or files you may want to return to, maintained by Windows 95 and Windows 98, Internet Explorer, America Online, and other programs.

finger: A program that displays information about someone on the Net. Used as a verb, finger means the act of getting info about someone on the Net by using the finger program.

firewall: A computer that connects a local network to the Internet and, for security reasons, lets only certain kinds of information in and out.

firewire: A very fast serial bus for connecting computer peripherals and video equipment. Also called *IEEE 1394.*

flame: To post angry, inflammatory, or insulting messages. When two or more individuals exchange a number of flames, we call it a flame war.

FTP: File Transfer Protocol, a method of transferring files from one computer to the other over the Net.

FTP server: A computer on the Internet that stores files for transmission by FTP.

GAK: Government Access to Keys, a U.S. government proposal to require that encryption software include a way for the government to break the code.

gateway: A computer that connects one network with another, where the two networks use different protocols.

GIF: Graphics Interchange Format, a patented type of graphics file originally defined by CompuServe and now found all over the Net. Files in this format end in .gif and are called *gif files* or just *gifs.*

gigabyte: One billion bytes or characters of data.

Gopher: An older Internet system that lets you find text information by using menus. Largely supplanted by the World Wide Web.

gov: When these letters appear as the last part of an address (for example, in cu.nih.gov), they indicate that the host computer is run by some government body, probably the U.S. federal government.

handle: A user's nickname or screen name.

header: The beginning of an e-mail message containing To and From addresses, the subject, the date, and other gobbledygook that's important to the programs that handle your mail. *See also* Part III.

hierarchy: The Usenet category to which a newsgroup belongs. The major hierarchies are `comp`, `rec`, `soc`, `sci`, `news`, `misc`, and `talk`, although hundreds more exist. *See also* Part IV.

home page: A Web page about a person or organization. *See also* Part VI.

host name: The name of a computer on the Internet, for example, `iecc.com`.

HTML: HyperText Markup Language, the language used to write pages for the World Wide Web. This language lets the text include codes that define fonts, layout, embedded graphics, and hypertext links. Don't worry: You don't have to know anything about it to use the World Wide Web. *See also* Part VI.

HTTP: HyperText Transfer Protocol, the way in which World Wide Web pages are transferred over the Net.

HTTPS: A variant of HTTP that encrypts messages for security.

hypertext: A system of writing and displaying text that enables the text to be linked in multiple ways, be available at several levels of detail, and contain links to related documents. The World Wide Web uses both hypertext and hypermedia, which adds other kinds of information, such as pictures, sound, and video. *See also* Part VI.

ICANN: Internet Corporation for Assigned Numbers and Names. A new nonprofit corporation created to administer top-level domains and precious IP addresses.

ICQ: I Seek You. A Web-based chat service. *See also* Part VIII.

IETF: Internet Engineering Task Force, the group that develops new technical standards for the Internet.

initialization string: The message your communications software sends to your modem to get it set up right. Your modem's manual should tell you what to use. If all else fails, use ATZ.

Internet: All the computers in the world talking to each other.

Internet Connection Wizard: Windows 98 and Windows 95 component that walks you through connecting to the Internet for the first time.

Internet Explorer: A popular Web browser from Microsoft that comes in Windows and Mac flavors. *See also* Part VI.

Internet Society: An organization dedicated to supporting the growth and evolution of the Internet. You can contact it at www.isoc.org.

InterNIC: The Internet Network Information Center, a central repository of information about the Internet. To register a domain name, *see* www.internic.net.

intranet: A private version of the Internet that lets people within an organization exchange data by using popular Internet tools, such as browsers.

IP: Internet Protocol. The rules computers use to send data over the Internet. *See* Part III for an explanation of IP addresses.

IRC: Internet Relay Chat, a system that enables Internet folks to talk to each other in real time (rather than after a delay, as with e-mail messages). *See also* Part VIII.

ISDN: Integrated Services Digital Network, a faster, digital phone service that operates at speeds of as much as 128 kilobits per second.

ISO: The International Organization for Standardization.

ISP: Internet Service Provider. The company that connects you to the Internet.

ITU-T: The International Telecommunications Union committee, which sets worldwide communication standards. *See also* www.itu.int.

Java: A computer language invented by Sun Microsystems. Java programs can run on any modern computer, making Java ideal for delivering application programs over the Internet.

JPEG: A type of still-image file found all over the Net. Files in this format end in .jpg or .jpeg and are called *jpeg* (pronounced "JAY-peg") *files*. Stands for Joint Photographic Experts Group.

K56flex: The Rockwell International modem technology for downloading data at 56,000 bps. Replaced by V.90.

Kermit: A file-transfer system developed at Columbia University and available for a variety of computers, from PCs to mainframes.

Key: A block of information used to create a unique pattern of encryption. *See also* Part IX.

kill file: A file that tells your newsreader which newsgroup articles you always want to skip. *See also* Part IV.

kilo-: Prefix meaning one thousand, though it's often used to mean 1,024 (2 to the tenth power) for computers.

LDAP: Lightweight Directory Access Protocol, a new Internet standard that lets applications access directory services.

link: A *hypertext* connection that can take you to another document or another part of the same document. On the *World Wide Web,* links appear as text or pictures that are highlighted. To follow a link, you click the highlighted material.

Linux: An *Open Source* version of the *UNIX* operating system that runs on personal computers and is supported by a dedicated band of enthusiasts on the Internet. (*See also* the www.linux.com and linuxnewbie.org Web sites or read the comp.os.linux.announce newsgroup.)

ListProc: A mailing list management program. *See also* Part V.

LISTSERV: A family of programs that automatically manages mailing lists, by distributing messages posted to the list and adding and deleting members, for example, which spares the list owner the tedium of having to do these tasks manually. The names of mailing lists maintained by LISTSERV often end with -L. *See also* Part V.

lurk: To read a Usenet newsgroup, mailing list, or chat group without posting any messages. Someone who lurks is a lurker. Lurking is okay.

Lynx: A character-based World Wide Web browser. No pictures, but fast. *See also* Part VI.

MacBinary: A file-encoding system that's popular among Macintosh users.

MacTCP: Component of the Mac operating system that connects your Mac to the Internet.

mail server: A computer on the Internet that provides mail services. *See also* Part V.

mailbot: A program that automatically sends or answers e-mail.

mailing list: A special kind of e-mail address that remails all incoming mail to a list of subscribers to the mailing list. Each mailing list has a specific topic, so you subscribe to the ones that interest you. *See also* Part V.

Majordomo: A program that handles mailing lists. *See also* Part V.

MBone: The multicast backbone. A special subnetwork on the Internet that supports live video and other multimedia.

megabyte: One million bytes or characters of data.

Microsoft Network (MSN): A commercial online service that provides many Internet services, including e-mail, Usenet newsgroups, and access to the World Wide Web.

MIDI: A way to transmit music as actual notes rather than as digitized sounds. Many electronic instruments have a MIDI output.

mil: When these letters appear as the last part of an address (the zone), they indicate that the host computer is run by some part of the U.S. military.

MIME: Multipurpose Internet Mail Extension. Used to send pictures, word processing files, and other nontext information through e-mail. *See also* Part III.

mirror: A Web server that provides copies of the same files as another server. Mirrors spread out the load for more popular Web sites.

modem: A gizmo that lets your computer talk on the phone or cable TV. Short for *mo*dulator–*dem*odulator. *See also* Part II.

moderator: The person who looks at the messages posted to a moderated mailing list or newsgroup before releasing them to the public. Moderators can nix messages that are stupid, redundant, wildly off the topic, or offensive, in their opinion.

MOO: *M*UD object-oriented; a MUD with programming capability. *See also MUD* and Part VIII.

MPEG: A type of video file found on the Net. Files in this format end in .mpg. Stands for Moving Picture Experts Group.

MP3: MPEG level 3. The audio component of *MPEG,* widely used to send music files over the Net. *See also* www.mp3.com.

MUD: Multi-User Dungeon, which started as a Dungeons and Dragons type of game that many people can play at one time; now, it's an Internet subculture. *See also* Part VIII.

net: A network, or (when capitalized) the Internet. When these letters appear as the last part of a host name (in www.abuse.net, for example), they indicate that the host computer is run by a networking organization, often an ISP.

Net Nanny: A program that tries to keep kiddies from accessing Web sites the company deems inappropriate.

Netscape: The maker of the popular Web *browser* Navigator that comes in Windows, Mac, and UNIX flavors. Now owned by AOL. *See also* Part VI.

network: Computers that are connected together. Those in the same or nearby buildings are called *Local-Area Networks;* those farther away are called *Wide-Area Networks;* when you interconnect networks all over the world, you get the Internet!

network computer (NC): A computer that lacks a hard disk and gets all its data instead over a computer network, such as the Internet.

newbie: A newcomer to the Internet (variant: clueless newbie). If you have read this book, of course, you're not a clueless newbie anymore!

news server: A computer on the Net that receives Usenet newsgroups and holds them so that you can read them. *See also* Part IV.

newsgroup: A topic area in the *Usenet* news system. *See also* Part IV.

newsreader: A program that lets you read and respond to the messages in Usenet newsgroups. *See also* Part IV.

nickname: The name by which you identify yourself when you're chatting. Also called *screen name* or *handle*. *See also* Part VIII.

node: A computer on the Internet, also called a *host.*

objects: Data and the computer programs that work with the data, all tied up with a ribbon so that other programs can use the objects without knowing what goes on inside.

Open Source: An approach to developing software where all the source code is published free of charge.

org: As the last part of a host name (in `www.uua.org`, for example), indicates that the host computer is run by a nonprofit organization, usually in the United States.

Outlook Express: The latest Microsoft e-mail and Usenet newsreading program. Not the same as Outlook, the e-mail program that comes with Microsoft Office. *See also* Parts III and IV.

packet: A chunk of information sent over a network. Each packet contains the address to which it's going and the address from which it came.

page: A document, or hunk of information, available by way of the *World Wide Web.* Each page can contain text, graphics files, sound files, video clips — you name it. *See also* Part VI.

parity: A simple system for checking for errors when data is transmitted from one computer to another. Just say "none" when you're setting up a communications program.

password: A secret code used to keep things private. Be sure to pick one that's not crackable, preferably two randomly chosen words separated by a number or special character. *Never* use a single word that is in a dictionary or any proper name.

PDF file: A method for distributing formatted documents over the Internet. You need a special reader program named Acrobat Reader. Get it at `www.adobe.com/acrobat`.

Perl: A popular but arcane language frequently used to make a Web *server* do neat things.

PGP: Phil's Pretty Good Privacy, a program that lets you encrypt and sign your e-mail. For more information, check in on the `comp.security.pgp.discuss` newsgroup or visit `web.mit.edu/network/pgp.html`. *See also* Part IX.

PICS: Platform for Internet Content Selection, a way of marking pages with ratings about what's inside. Designed to keep kids from getting at the racy stuff, although it has other applications too. *See also* Part VI.

Pine: A popular UNIX-based mail program. Pine is easy to use (for a UNIX program). *See also* Part III.

ping: To send a short message to which another computer automatically responds. If you can't ping the other computer, you probably can't talk to it any other way either.

PKZIP: A file-compression program that runs on PCs. PKZIP creates a *ZIP file* that contains compressed versions of one or more files. To restore these files to their former size and shape, you use PKUNZIP, ZipMagic, or WinZip.

plug-in: A computer program you add to your browser to help it handle a special type of file. *See also* Part VI.

POP: Post Office Protocol, a system by which a mail server on the Internet lets you pick up your e-mail and download it to your PC or Mac. Also called *POP3*. *See also* Part III.

port number: An identifying number assigned to each program that is chatting on the Internet. You hardly ever have to know these numbers — the Internet programs work this stuff out among themselves.

PPP: Point-to-Point Protocol, a scheme for connecting your computer to the Internet over a phone line. Like *SLIP,* only better. Most dial-up Internet accounts use PPP.

protocol: The agreed-on rules that computers rely on to talk among themselves. A set of signals that mean "go ahead," "got it," "didn't get it, please resend," "all done," and so on.

public-key cryptography: A method for sending secret messages whereby you get two keys: a public key you give out freely so that people can send you coded messages and a second, private key that decodes them. *See also* Part IX.

push: A type of technology that sends information you may want to your computer as soon as it's available, without your specific request.

QuickTime: A video file format invented by Apple Computer and widely used on the Net.

RealAudio: A popular streaming-audio file format that lets you listen to programs over the Net. You can get a player plug-in at www.real.com.

RC4: A simple but powerful encryption algorithm developed by Ron Rivest and widely used on the Internet. *See also* ciphersaber.gurus.com.

RFC: Request for Comment, a numbered series of documents that specify how the different parts of the Internet work. For example, RFC-822 describes the Internet e-mail message format.

router: A computer that connects two or more *networks.*

RSA: A popular, patented, *public-key cryptography* system. *See also* Part IX.

RTFM: Read The Manual, a suggestion made by people who feel that you have wasted their time by asking a question you could have found the answer to by looking it up in an obvious place. A well-known and much-used FTP site named rtfm.mit.edu contains FAQs for all Usenet newsgroups.

SDMI: Secure Digital Music Initiative. The recording industry's alternative to the popular MP3 format. SDMI files cannot be shared.

search engine: A program used to search for things on the *World Wide Web.* An example of a publicly available search engine is *AltaVista.*

secure server: A Web server that uses encryption to prevent others from reading messages to or from your browser, such as ordering information.

serial port: The place in back of your computer where you plug in your *modem.* Also called a *communications port* or *comm port.*

server: A computer that provides a service — such as e-mail, Web data, Usenet, or FTP — to another computer or computers (known as *clients*) on a network.

shareware: Computer programs that are easily available for you to try with the understanding that, if you decide to keep the program, you will send the requested payment to the shareware provider specified in the program. It's an honor system. A great deal of good stuff is available, and people's voluntary compliance makes it viable.

Shockwave: A standard for viewing interactive multimedia on the World Wide Web. For a copy of the Shockwave plug-in for your browser, visit www.macromedia.com/shockwave.

SLIP: Serial Line Internet Protocol, a software scheme for connecting your computer to the Internet over a serial line. Obsolete and replaced by *PPP.*

smiley: A combination of special characters that portray emotions, such as : -) or : - (. Hundreds have been invented, although only a few are in active use. *See also* Part III for a list.

S/MIME: Secure Multipurpose Internet Mail Extension. An extension to MIME that includes encryption. *See also* Part III.

SMTP: Simple Mail Transfer Protocol, the misnamed method by which Internet mail is delivered from one computer to another.

soc: A type of newsgroup that discusses social topics, covering subjects from `soc.men` to `soc.religion.buddhist` to `soc.culture.canada`. *See also* Part IV.

socket: A logical "port" a program uses to connect to another program running on another computer on the Internet. You may have an FTP program using sockets for its FTP session, for example, while Eudora connects by way of another socket to get your mail.

spam: The act of sending e-mail to thousands of uninterested recipients or of posting inappropriate messages to many uninterested newsgroups or mailing lists. It's antisocial and ineffective. *See also* Part III.

SSL: Secure Socket Layer, a technology that lets one computer verify another's identity and allow secure connections.

stop bit: Just say "1" when you're setting up your communications software.

streaming audio: A system for sending sound files over the Net that starts playing the sound before the sound file finishes downloading, which lets you listen with minimal delay. *RealAudio* is the most popular.

surf: To wander around the World Wide Web, looking for interesting stuff.

T1: A telecommunications standard that carries 24 voice calls or data at 1.44 million bps over a pair of telephone lines.

TCP/IP: The way networks communicate with each other on the Internet. Stands for Transfer Control Protocol/Internet Protocol.

telnet: A program that lets you log in to other computers on the Net. *See also* Part IX.

terminal: In the olden days, a computer terminal consisted of just a screen and a keyboard. If you have a personal computer and you want to connect to a big computer somewhere, you can run a program that makes it *pretend* to be a brainless terminal. The program is called a *terminal emulator, terminal program,* or *communications program.*

text file: A file that contains only textual characters, with no special formatting, graphical information, sound clips, video, or what-have-you. Most computers, other than some IBM mainframes, store their text by using a system of codes named *ASCII,* so these files are also known as *ASCII text files. See also* Unicode.

thread: An article posted to a Usenet newsgroup, together with all the follow-up articles, the follow-ups to follow-ups, and so on. *See also* Part IV.

TLD: *T*op-*l*evel *d*omain. Another term for *zone.*

UDP: User Datagram Protocol, a system used for applications to send quick, one-shot messages to each other.

Unicode: An up-and-coming extension of ASCII that attempts to include the characters of all active written languages.

UNIX: A geeky operating system originally developed by Bell Labs and widely used for Internet servers. (Check out a copy of *UNIX For Dummies,* 4th Edition, by John R. Levine and Margaret Levine Young, published by IDG Books Worldwide, Inc.).

upload: To put your stuff on somebody else's computer.

URI: Universal Resource Identifier, a generalized version of a URL (and the one that Tim Berners-Lee, the inventor of the Web, prefers).

URL: Uniform Resource Locator, a standardized way of naming network resources, used for linking pages together on the World Wide Web. *See also* Part VI.

URN: Uniform Resource Name, a Web page name that doesn't change when the page is moved to a different computer, proposed as a solution to the broken-link problem.

USB: Universal Serial Bus. A connection for keyboards, mice, modems, printers, and scanners used on many new PCs and the iMac.

Usenet: A system of thousands of newsgroups. You read the messages by using a **newsreader.**

uuencode/uudecode: Programs that enable you to send binary files as e-mail.

viewer: A program used by Internet client programs to show you files that contain stuff other than text.

virtual reality: A 3-D visual computer simulation that responds to your input so realistically that you feel as though you're inside another world.

virus: Program that adds itself to ("infects") another program or document and then creates copies of itself to infect others. Some viruses travel over the Internet, carried by programs or documents attached to e-mail.

V.nn: Series of recommendations from the *ITU-T* for data communication. *See also* "Modem Specs," in Part II.

VRML: A language used for building *virtual reality* pages on the World Wide Web. *See also* Part VI.

VT100: The model number of a *terminal* made in the early 1980s by Digital Equipment Corporation. Some computers on the Internet expect to talk to VT100-type terminals, which most communication programs can emulate.

WAIS: *W*ide-*a*rea *i*nformation *s*ervers, an older information search system, now supplanted by the World Wide Web.

WAV: A popular format for sound files (.wav files) found on the Internet.

Web page: A document available on the World Wide Web. *See also* Part VI.

Winsock: A standard way for Windows programs to work with TCP/IP. You use it if you directly connect your Windows PC to the Internet, with either a permanent connection or a modem by using PPP.

WinZip: A file-compression program that runs under Windows. It reads and creates a ZIP file that contains compressed versions of one or more files.

World Wide Web (WWW): A hypermedia system that lets you browse through lots of interesting information. The Web is the central repository of humanity's information in the 21st century. *See also* Part VI.

x2: USRobotics modem technology for downloading data at 56,000 bps. Replaced by *V.90*.

X.400: A cumbersome, *ITU*-blessed mail standard that competes with the Internet SMTP mail standard.

X.500: A standard for white-pages e-mail directory services. It isn't quite as broken as X.400, and Internet people are trying to use it.

X.509: A standard for storing the information needed to validate electronic signatures, also called a *certificate* or *cert*.

xDSL: A family of methods for sending data at high speed over phone wires. *See also* ADSL.

XML: Extensible Markup Language. A more powerful replacement for *HTML*.

Xmodem: A protocol for sending files between computers; the second choice after *Zmodem.*

XON/XOFF: One way for your computer to say "Wait a sec!" when data is coming in too fast; the other way is usually called *hardware flow control.*

Yahoo!: A set of Web pages that provide a subject-oriented guide to the World Wide Web. Go to the URL www.yahoo.com/. *See also* Part VI.

ZIP file: An *archive* that has been compressed by using PKZIP, WinZip, ZipMagic, or a compatible program.

Zmodem: A protocol for sending files between computers, better than **Xmodem**.

zone: The last part of an Internet host name. Also called a *top-level domain name* or *TLD. See also* Part III and the appendix.

Index

Symbols

<> (angle brackets), 161
* (asterisk), 105, 134, 173
@ (at sign), 32, 50, 141, 173–174
\ (backslash), 173
: (colon), 90
, (comma), 32
"" (double quotes), 104
/ (forward slash), 89–90, 138–140, 161, 173
- (hyphen), 89, 104
() (parentheses), 32, 105
+ (plus sign), 104
? (question mark), 63
> (right-arrow sign), 43, 44, 48, 52
~ (tilde), 89, 92, 173
| (vertical bar), 52

A

abbreviations, 26, 128–129
About.com, 104
acronyms, 26
ActiveX controls (Microsoft), 81, 84–86, 181
Adobe Acrobat, 84, 85, 190
AfterDinner, 109
AIFF files, 118
AIM (AOL Instant Messenger), 124, 132–133
airlines, 113
Alert Link Runner for Windows, 163
algorithms, 153–154
aliases, 48
AltaVista, 13, 30
  basic description of, 103, 181
  power searching with, 104–105
Amazon.com, 113, 167
American Surrogacy Center, 116

angle brackets (<>), 161
anonymizer Web site, 87
AOL (America Online)
  basic description of, 38–41, 181
  browsing the Web with, 81, 92–94
  chat, 21, 124, 126–127, 130–135
  contact information for, 21
  creating a home page with, 159, 165
  e-mail with, 29, 36–41
  filtering features, 83–84
  FTP and, 170
  Instant Messenger (AIM), 124, 132–133
  as a leading online service, 20
  Personal Filing Cabinet, 41
  reading newsgroups with, 66
  software, 23
  Web site, 92
apples, shopping for, 115
archives, 75, 118–119, 182. *See also* compression
ARPA (Advanced Research Projects Agency), 6, 182
ASCII (American Standard Code for Information Interchange), 170, 171, 182
asterisk (*), 105, 134, 173
at sign (@), 32, 50, 141, 173–174
AT&T (American Telephone & Telegraph), 21
attachments, 27, 37, 40
  basic description of, 182
  Eudora and, 44–45
  infected with viruses, 121
  Netscape Messenger and, 52
  Outlook Express and, 55
  Pine and, 57–58
auctions, 110–111
AutoByTel, 116
autocomplete features, 91
automobiles, shopping for, 116

B

backslash (\), 173
backup systems, 16
Barnes and Noble, 113
Baroudi, Carol, 31, 155
BBEdit Lite, 164
Bcc (blind carbon copy), 28, 31, 182
Bell Labs, 194
Berners-Lee, Tim, 79
Better Telnet for Macintosh, 172
BinHex, 37, 45, 182
Blue Moon Review, 109
bonds, 115
bookmarks, 94, 95–96, 99–100,
    106, 183
booksellers, 113
Borders.com, 113
The Boston Globe Web site, 110
bots (robots), 28, 143
bps (bits per second), 17, 182, 183
Britannica.com, 107
brokerage houses, 115
browser(s). *See also* Internet
    Explorer browser; Netscape
    Navigator browser
  AOL, 81, 92–94
  autocomplete features, 91
  basic description of, 23, 80, 183
  bookmark features, 94, 95–96, 99–
    100, 106, 183
  displaying HTML code with, 164–165
  home page settings for, 93, 95, 99
  Java applets and, 158
  Lynx browser, 81, 96–98, 188
  navigating the Web with, 81–82
  PPP accounts and, 22
  problems with, troubleshooting,
    88–90
  security and, 86–88, 152–153
  shell accounts and, 22
Buddy Lists, 134
businesses, starting, on the Web,
    167–168
busy signals, 88

C

cable Internet service, 10–11, 18
cable modems, 10–11, 18
Cable News Network, 110
call waiting, 20
Caller ID, 12
camcorders, digital, 15
capitalization, 36, 89, 91, 104, 105
Carfax, 116
cars, shopping for, 116
cartridge tapes, 16
case-sensitivity, 36, 89, 91, 104, 105
Cc (carbon copy), 31, 183
CDNow.com, 115
CDs, shopping for, 115–116
censorship, 21, 82–84
Census Bureau, 108
channels, 82, 124, 137–143, 183
Charles Schwab Online, 115
chat
  AOL, 21, 124, 126–127, 130–135
  basic description of, 123–148, 183
  conversations, getting started
    with, 125–126
  etiquette, 126–127
  private, 133, 142, 143
  problems with, reporting, 127,
    129, 132
  profiles, 126, 130, 133
  rooms, searching for specific, 130–131
  safe and healthy, guidelines for,
    127–128
  Web-based, 124, 144
children, safety issues related to,
    82–84, 127
CIA World Factbook, 107, 175
CitySearch, 115
Clear Phone (Engineering
    Consulting), 147
clothing, shopping for, 115
collectibles, 113–114
colon (:), 90
comma (,), 32
complaints, filing, 132, 143

compression, 37, 83–85, 117–120.
    See also archives
CompuServe
  acquisition of, by AOL, 20
  basic description of, 183
  contact information for, 21
  e-mail addresses, 32, 36–37
  FTP and, 170
  software, 23
  telnet and, 172
  Web hosting, 159
computers
  free, 15
  investing in, 15–17
  laptop, 11, 15, 18
  network (NCs), 13–14, 157–159, 189
  new models of, 15
  remote, connecting to, 172
  secondhand, 14
  upgrading, 17
Condom Country, 113
conference calls, 146
contact lists, 135–136
conventions, used in this book, 3–4
cookies, 86–87, 184
copyrights, 107, 109, 163
country codes, 34–35, 175–180, 184
crashes, 90. *See also* troubleshooting
credit cards, 86, 116–117, 152, 167
cross-posting, 63, 66
cryptography, 150–157, 184, 191,
    192. *See also* encryption
cybercafés, 13, 30
CyberPatrol, 83, 184
Cybersitter, 83

D

Datek Online Broker, 115
dating resources, 114
decoding files, 117–120
Deja.com, 30, 104, 116
  basic description of, 60–61
  reading newsgroups with, 67–68
  setting up a discussion group at, 66

deleting
  bookmarks, 99
  e-mail, 57
  parts of e-mail messages, 55
Dial-Up Networking, 23, 184
Diffie-Hellman (D-H) cryptography,
    153, 184. *See also* cryptography
DigiPhone, 147
digital
  IDs, 157
  watermarks, 109
direct connections, to the Internet, 12
directories. *See* folders
disk space, 16, 107
DNS (domain name server), 34,
    88–90, 184
dolls, shopping for, 113–114
domain names, 33–34, 184. *See also*
    DNS (domain name server)
DOS (Disk Operating System), 23, 45
double quotes (""), 104
downloading files, 118, 171, 184
DropStuff with Expander Enhancer,
    85, 118
DSL (Digital Subscriber Line), 10–12,
    14, 15, 18

E

eBay, 110
education Web sites, 114
Eisen, Lewis S., 62
e-mail. *See also* attachments; e-mail
    addresses
  abbreviations, 26
  acronyms, 26
  advantages of, 6
  aliases, 48
  basic description of, 25–58, 184
  Bcc (blind carbon copy), 28, 31, 182
  Cc (carbon copy), 31, 183
  chain letters, 28
  chat and, comparison of, 124
  composing, 46–47
  etiquette, 26–27
  filtering features, 78

e-mail *(continued)*
  forwarding, 28, 41, 44, 48, 52, 56–58
  free, 13
  getting incoming, 42, 50–51, 53–54
  headers, 30–31, 186
  reading, 38–44, 46, 50–51, 53–54, 57
  rejected (bounced), 31
  replying to, 41, 43–44, 47–48, 52,
    55–58
  saving, 41, 47–49, 52–53, 56, 58
  security and, 153–156
  sending, 39–40, 43, 46–47, 51–58
  signatures, 40
  software, 23–24
  spam (junk e-mail), 28, 39, 193
  time taken up by reading, 8
  voice, 147
e-mail address(es). *See also* e-mail
  for the authors of this book, 4
  basic description of, 32–38
  books, 48
  finding, 29–30, 38–39
  newsgroups and, 60–61
  used with mailing lists, 72–73
E-Mail For Dummies, 2nd Edition
  (Baroudi, Levine, Levine
  Young, and Reinhold), 31, 156
emoticons, 37–38, 128–129
employment resources, 114
encryption, 87–88, 150–157. *See*
  also cryptography
  basic description of, 184
  PGP (Pretty Good Privacy), 7, 42,
    153–157, 191
Encyclopedia Britannica, 107
Enhanced CU-SeeMe (White Pine
  Software), 147
EntryPoint, 110
error messages, 88–90
e-stamp.com, 115
Ethernet, 10–11, 15, 16, 184
etiquette
  chat, 126–127
  e-mail, 26–27
  newgroup, 62–63
E*Trade, 115

Eudora, 22, 24, 78
  basic description of, 41–45, 185
  highlighting of URLs in, 81
Eudora Light, 41
Eudora Pro, 41–42, 45
Excel (Microsoft), 120
Excite, 103
ezines, 109

F

FAQs (Frequently Asked Questions), 61, 63–64, 143, 185, 192
Fast Search, 103
favorites lists, 94, 95–96, 185
fax transmissions, 6, 107
FBI (Federal Bureau of Investigation), 151
feedback, 4, 110–111
Fetch for Macintosh, 170
Fidelity Investments, 115
file(s)
  compression, 37, 83–85, 117–120
  decoding, 117–120
  navigating, 170–171
  -name extensions, 91, 118, 119, 160
  "not found" errors, 89–90
  opening, 82
  uncompressing, 117–120
filtering, 66, 78, 82–84
finger, 173–174, 185
fingerprints, 155
flame, 27, 185
Flash Sessions, 39
floppy disks, 16
florists, 114
folders
  creating new, 53
  navigating, 170–171
  saving e-mail in, 48–49, 51–53, 56
fonts, used in this book, 3–4
...For Dummies Web site, 4
forms, 82
forward slash (/), 89–90, 138–140,
  161, 173
Free Agent, 70

free computers, 15
free services, 13, 106–107
  e-mail, 13, 30
  fax transmissions, 107
  telephone service, 107
Free Software Foundation, 119
Freedrive, 107
Freeserve, 13
freeware, 111–112
FTP (File Transfer Protocol), 24, 35, 91, 182
  basic description of, 170–171, 185
  file compression and, 117
  servers, 170, 185

G

GeoCities, 159
geographical names (country codes), 34–35, 175–180, 184
GIF (Graphics Interchange Format), 118–119, 185. *See also* graphics
gigabytes, 16, 185
GNU project, 119
Go Net-Wide, 165
Goldberg, Ian, 151
Google, 103
gopher, 91, 185
graphics
  disabling, 88
  GIF (Graphics Interchange Format), 118–119, 185
  JPEG (Joint Photographics Expert Group), 119, 187
  using, in your Web page, 162, 163
Great Tapes for Kids, 115–116
groceries, 114
gunzip, 119
.gz files, 119
gzip, 119

H

handles, 124, 186
hard disk space, 16, 107
headers, 30–31, 186

Heavens Above, 108
helper programs, 84–86
History list, 96
home page(s). *See also* Web pages
  basic description of, 186
  browser settings for, 93, 95, 99
  creating your own, 159–163
home buying, 114
host names, 32, 33–34, 90, 186
Hot Dog Web Editor, 164
.hqx files, 119
HTML (HyperText Markup Language)
  authoring/editing, 80, 160–165
  basic description of, 186
  files, filename extensions for, 91
  format, saving Web pages in, 82
  tags, 161–162
HTTP (HyperText Transfer Protocol), 91, 186
HushMail, 30, 155
hyphen (-), 89, 104

I

iBook, 15
icons, used in this book, 3
ICQ (I Seek You), 124, 135–137, 186
I-drive Web site, 107
IETF (Internet Engineering Task Force), 6, 186
iMac, 15
Info-Mac archive, 112
information sources, 107–108
Infoseek, 30, 103
Internet
  basic description of, 6, 186
  economy, hooking up to, 12–14
  getting to know, 5–8
  history of, 6
  services provided by, summary of, 8
  telephony, 146–147
  what's so great about the, 6–7
Internet Connection Wizard, 23, 186
Internet Domain Registrars, 34

Internet Explorer browser. *See also*
　browsers
　basic description of, 80–81, 186
　cookie settings, 87
　cryptography and, 152–153
　using, 94–96
Internet For Dummies, 7th Edition,
　(Baroudi, Levine, Levine
　Young), 31
Internet For Dummies Central, 33
Internet For Dummies QR Web site, 4
Internet Phone (VocalTec), 147
Internet Society, 6, 187
IP (Internet Protocol), 34, 187
Iphone, 147
IRC (Internet Relay Chat), 124, 137–
　143, 187
IRcle, 137, 138, 140–141
ISA slots, 16
ISDN (Integrated Services Digital
　Network), 10, 12, 187
ISDN For Dummies, 2nd Edition
　(Angell), 12
ISPs (Internet Service Providers)
　advantages of, 21–22
　basic description of, 21–22, 187
　cable Internet access and, 11
　chat services provided by, 125, 129
　connection software and, 23
　Linux and, 15
　lists of, 114
　modems recommended by, 17
　news servers belonging to, 68
　selecting, 20–22
　set-top boxes and, 14
ITU (International Telecommunica-
　tions Union), 17, 147, 187

J

Java, 82, 92, 144, 157–159, 187
Java For Dummies, 3rd Edition
　(Walsh), 158

Java Programming For Dummies,
　3rd Edition (Koosis and
　Koosis), 158
JavaScript, 158
JavaScript For Dummies, 2nd
　Edition (Vander Veer), 158
job listings, 114
Joker Web site, 34
JPEG (Joint Photographics Expert
　Group), 119, 187. *See also*
　graphics
Juno, 13, 30, 45–46

K

Kbps (kilobit per second), 17
keystroke commands, 97–98
kids, safety issues related to,
　82–84, 127

L

LANs (Local Area Networks),
　46, 189
laptop computers, 11, 15, 18
libraries, public, 6, 13, 30, 106, 107
Library of Congress, 107
link(s). *See also* URLs (Uniform
　Resource Locators)
　exchanges, 166
　basic description of, 80, 188
　following, 93, 95, 99
　highlighting of, 81, 97
Linux, 15, 49–53, 56–58, 80
　basic description of, 188
　telnet and, 172–173
ListProc, 72, 75, 76, 188
LISTSERV, 72, 75, 76, 188
literature, online sources of, 107, 109
Lycos, 103, 109
Lynx browser, 81, 96–98, 188. *See
　also* browsers
Lyris, 72

M

Macintosh
  basic description of, 15
  browsers for, 80
  chat software, 137
  ISPs and, 22
  newsreaders, 70
  software archives, 112
  using Eudora with, 41–45
  using Outlook Express with, 53–56
Macromedia Shockwave, 86
MacTCP, 171–172, 188
magazines, 109
The Mail Archive, 104
Mailbase, 72, 76
mailing list(s)
  basic description of, 71–79, 188
  digested, receiving, 75
  finding, 73
  moderated, 72
  open and closed, 74–75
  sending messages to, 75
  servers, 72
  special requests to, 76–77
  starting your own, 77
  subscribing and unsubscribing to,
    73–74
  Web-based, 72, 74
mailto: links, 91
Majordomo, 72, 75, 76, 188
MapQuest, 108
maps, 107–108
Match.com, 114
Mbps (megabit per second), 17
memory, 16–17, 117
<META> tag, 162, 163, 166
MetaCrawler, 104, 106
MetaSpy, 106
Microsoft Web site, 80, 95, 120
MIME (Multipurpose Internet Mail
    Extension), 37, 40, 44–45,
    118, 189
minus sign, 105
mIRC, 137–138, 140–141
mirror (duplicate) sites, 88, 112, 189

modems, 14, 15, 146, 159
  basic description of, 17–20, 189
  cable modems, 10–11, 18
  problems with, 88
  specs for, 17–18
Modems For Dummies, 3rd Edition
    (Rathbone), 17
monitors, color, 16
MOOs, 144–146, 171, 189
MP3 (MPEG level 3), 109, 118–119,
    189
MP3.com, 109
MP3Now, 109
MPEG (Moving Picture Experts
    Group), 109, 118, 189
MSN (Microsoft Network), 21, 30,
    188
MSNBC, 110
MUDs (Multi-User Dungeons), 144–
    146, 171, 189
music, 109–110, 115–116, 118–119, 189
musical instruments, shopping
    for, 116
Musser Xylophones, 116
My Yahoo!, 110
MyTalk Web site, 107

N

National Public Radio, 159
National Science Foundation, 6
Neptune's Joinery, 116
Net Nanny, 83, 189
NetMeeting (Microsoft), 147
Netscape Communicator, 80, 87.
    See also Netscape Messenger;
    Netscape
Netscape Messenger, 49–53, 153
Netscape Navigator browser. *See
    also* browsers
  basic description of, 80–81, 189
  cryptography and, 152–153
  using, 98–100
Netscape Newsgroup, 68
Netscape Web site, 80
NetTerm for Windows, 172

network computers (NCs), 13–14,
  157–159, 189
network news. *See* newsgroups
Network Solutions, 33–34
NetZero, 13
The New York Times Web site, 110
newbies, 190
news servers, 68, 190
newsgroup(s)
  articles, replying to, 68
  basic description of, 59–70, 190
  finding someone who has posted
    messages in, 30
  hierarchies, 61–62
  information about IRC in, 143
  moderated, 64–65
  names, 61–62
  netiquette, 62–63
  port numbers for, 36
  posting articles in, 64–65, 68
  reading, 66–70
  shopping resources in, 112–113
  starting your own, 65–66
newspapers, 7, 108, 110
nicknames, 124, 141–142, 190
NuBus slots, 16

0

Official U.S. Gazetteer, 108
On The Air, Inc., 159
Online Book Initiatives, 107
online chat. *See* chat
online services. *See also* AOL
    (America Online; CompuServe;
    MSN (Microsoft Network)
  basic description of, 20–21
  filtering features provided by, 83–84
organizational names, 34–35
Outlook Express (Microsoft)
  basic description of, 24, 190
  filtering features, 78
  reading newsgroups with, 69–70
  security and, 153
  using, 53–56

P

parental controls, 82–84
parentheses, 32, 105
passwords, 83, 155, 157, 172
  basic description of, 190
  cookies and, 86
PCI slots, 16
PCMCIA card modems, 18
PDF (Portable Document Format),
    85, 190
Personal Filing Cabinet, 41
PGP (Pretty Good Privacy) encryp-
    tion, 7, 42, 153–157, 191
Pine (e-mail program), 22,
    56–58, 191
PKUNZIP, 120
PKZIP, 120, 191
plug-ins, 81, 84–86, 100, 159, 191
plus sign (+), 104
POP (Post Office Protocol),
    49–50, 191
pornography, 82–84
port numbers, 35–36, 191
portals, 102–104
postal mail (snail mail), 6, 115
postmasters, 31
PPP accounts, 22–23, 49, 170–171, 191
printers, 16
privacy, 86–88, 133, 142–143. *See
    also* security
processors, 17, 159
Prodigy, 20
profiles, chat, 126, 130, 133
proxy servers, 13
public-key cryptography, 156–157,
    191. *See also* encryption
PureMp3, 109

Q

question mark (?), 63
QuickTime, 15, 86, 118, 159, 192

R

radio, 18, 159
Radio Shack, 20
RAM (random-access memory),
    16–17, 117
real estate, 114
RealGuide, 159
RealPlayer, 85, 159
Reel.com, 115
regional information providers, 108
remote computers, connecting to, 172
restaurant listings, 115
right-arrow sign (>), 43, 44, 48, 52
rippers, 109
robots, 28, 143
RSA public-key cryptography, 152,
    153–154, 192

S

SafeSurf, 83
San Jose Mercury News Web site, 110
satellites, 108
saving
    e-mail, 41, 47–49, 52–53, 56, 58
    newsgroup articles, 67
    Web pages, 82
screen names
    basic description of, 124
    choosing, 127, 131–132
    ignoring, 126, 129, 130
SDMI (Secure Digital Music
    Initiative), 109, 192
search engines
    basic description of, 102–106, 192
    finding e-mail addresses with, 30
    power searches with, 104–105
    strategies for using, 105–106
secondhand computers, 14
security. *See also* encryption;
    passwords; privacy
    basic description of, 86–88, 150–157
    browser settings for, 86–87

credit card sales and, 86,
    116–117, 152
servers and, 152, 192
servers
    basic description of, 192
    DNS, 34, 88–90, 184
    FTP, 170, 185
    Linux and, 15
    news, 68, 190
    POP, 49–50
    problems with, 88–90
    proxy, 13
    secure, 152, 192
    SMTP, 42, 49, 50, 193
set-top boxes, 14
Sex For Dummies (Westheimer), 128
shareware, 111–112, 121, 192
Shareware.com, 111–112
shell accounts, 22
Shoenhof's Foreign Books, 113
shopping online
    basic description of, 112–117
    recommended Web sites for, 112–116
Sidewalk.com, 115
.sit files, 119
A Small Garlic Press, 109
smileys, 27, 37–38, 128–129, 193
SMTP (Simple Mail Transfer
    Protocol), 42, 49, 50, 193
software (Internet access)
    AOL, 23
    basic description of, 14–15, 22–24
    CompuServe, 23
    e-mail, 23–24
SoundApp, 109
sounds, in chat rooms, 134–135
spam, 28, 39, 193
Speak Freely, 147
spelling, 27, 40–41, 47–48, 55, 63–64
Sprint, 21
Stamps.com, 115
statistics, 108
stocks, 115
StuffIt Expander, 85, 118, 119, 120
Submit It, 165
submittal services, 165–166

Suite 101, 104
Sun Microsystems, 157, 158
surfing
  basic description of, 80, 193
  privacy issues and, 86–88
  tips and ideas, 106
SurfWatch, 83
surrogacy programs, 116
Switchboard Webmail, 30

T

.tar files, 119
TCP/IP (Transmission Control
    Protocol/Internet Protocol),
    170, 193
telephone
  directories ("white pages"), 29, 117
  disadvantages of using, 6
  lines, 14, 19–20, 88
  service, free, 107
telephony, 146–147
television, 14, 159
Telirati, 147
telnet, 24, 171–173, 193
Terraserver (Microsoft), 108
threads, 64, 194
tilde (~), 89, 92, 173
time, world, 108
TLDs (top-level domains), 33,
    34–35, 194, 196
TOSSpam, 39
Tripod, 159
trolls, 63
troubleshooting, 88–90
T. Rowe Price, 115
TUCOWS (The Ultimate Collection
    of Winsock Software), 98, 100,
    112, 137

U

The Ultimate Collection of Winsock
    Software (TUCOWS), 98, 100,
    112, 137

uncompressing files, 117–120. *See
    also* compression
United Nations, 108
UNIX, 15, 119
  basic description of, 194
  browsers, 80, 81, 96–97
  chat and, 137
  e-mail and, 49–53, 56–58
  finger and, 173–174
  FTP and, 170, 171
  learning more about, 22, 173
  shell accounts and, 22
  telnet and, 172–173
Upgrading and Fixing PCs, 3rd
    Edition (Rathbone), 17
uploading, 171, 194
URLs (Uniform Resource Loca-
    tors). *See also* links
  basic description of, 36, 80,
    90–92, 194
  entering, 89, 91
  forms and, 82
  power searching and, 104
  in printed sources, 89
  security and, 87
  temporary, 90
  for your own Web page, 162, 163
U.S. Census Bureau, 108
U.S. Department of Justice, 80
U.S. Library of Congress, 107
U.S. Naval Observatory, 108
USA.NET Net@ddress, 30
Usenet newsgroups. *See*
    newsgroups
uuencoding, 37, 45, 194

V

Vander Veer, Emily, 158
VeriSign, 153–154, 157
vertical bar (|), 52
video phones, 147
viruses, 54, 118, 120–121, 195
VitaminShoppe.com, 116
voice mail, 147
Voice on the Net, 147

W

Wagner, David, 151
The Wall Street Journal Web site, 110
Walsh, Aaron E., 158
WAV files, 118, 134–135, 195
Web browsers. *See* browsers
Web directories, 102–106
Web page(s). *See also* browsers;
    home pages; Web sites
  creating your own, 159–163
  designers, finding, 116
  maintenance, 163–164
  publicizing, 165–166
  reloading, 93
  saving, 82
  tips for effective, 162–163
  viewing, 92–93, 95, 98–99
Web sites. *See also* specific sites;
    Web pages
  basic description of, 80, 190, 195
  mirror (duplicate) sites, 88, 112, 189
  overloaded, 88, 89
Webcrawler, 103
Webmaster, 80
WebPromote, 165
Webrings, 104, 166
WebTV, 14
Westheimer, Ruth, 128
"white page" directories, 29, 117
whiteboards, 146
WinAMP, 109
Windows (Microsoft), 12, 15
  browsers for, 80
  connection software, 23
  software archives, 112
  using Eudora with, 41–45
  using Juno with, 45–49
  using Netscape Messenger with,
    49–53
  using Outlook Express with, 53–56
Winsock, 170, 171–172, 195
WinZip, 37, 84–85, 118–120, 195
WMA (Windows Media Audio)
    format, 109

Word (Microsoft), 37, 120
World Wide Web. *See also* Web
    pages; Web sites
  ABCs of, 80–81
  basic description of, 79–100, 195
  finding your way around, 81–82
  port number for, 35
  world time, 108
WS_FTP, 170, 171

X

Xerox PARC Map Server, 108

Y

Yahoo!
  Auctions, 111
  basic description of, 103, 196
  Broadcast, 159
  chat information, 144
  company listings, 16
  directory of free Internet access
    services, 13
  finding Web page designers
    through, 116
  local information, 108
  Mail, 30
  People Search, 29
  submittal service listings, 165
  as a Web directory, 102
yiddish, 116

Z

.z files, 119
.Z files, 120
zip files, 120, 196
ZipMagic, 37, 84–85, 118
zones (TLDs), 33, 34–35, 194, 196
The Zuzu's Petals Literary Resource,
    109

IDG BOOKS WORLDWIDE BOOK REGISTRATION

Register This Book and Win!

We want to hear from you!

Visit **http://my2cents.dummies.com** to register this book and tell us how you liked it!

- ✔ Get entered in our monthly prize giveaway.

- ✔ Give us feedback about this book — tell us what you like best, what you like least, or maybe what you'd like to ask the author and us to change!

- ✔ Let us know any other ...*For Dummies*® topics that interest you.

Your feedback helps us determine what books to publish, tells us what coverage to add as we revise our books, and lets us know whether we're meeting your needs as a ...*For Dummies* reader. You're our most valuable resource, and what you have to say is important to us!

Not on the Web yet? It's easy to get started with *Dummies 101*®: *The Internet For Windows*® *98* or *The Internet For Dummies*,® 6th Edition, at local retailers everywhere.

Or let us know what you think by sending us a letter at the following address:

...*For Dummies* Book Registration
Dummies Press
10475 Crosspoint Blvd.
Indianapolis, IN 46256

BESTSELLING
BOOK SERIES